BEGINNING WITH FREUD

The Classical Schools
of
Psychotherapy

by John H. Morgan, Ph.D., D.Sc., Psy.D.

Karl Mannheim Professor of the
History and Philosophy of the Social Sciences
Graduate Theological Foundation
Sir Julian Huxley Research Professor
Cloverdale College
Senior Fellow of Foundation House/Oxford
Member of the Advisory Board
Centre for the Study of Religion in Public Life
Oxford University
Summer Tutor, International Programs
Oxford University
Summer Tutor, Madingley Hall
Cambridge University

The Classical Schools
of Psychotherapy

John H. Morgan
Ph.D.(Hartford), D.Sc.(London), Psy.D.

Library of Congress
LOC 2009943623

ISBN 1-55605-399-1
978-155605-3993

Wyndham Hall Press
5050 Kerr Rd.
Lima, Oh 45806

ACKNOWLEDGMENTS

I have spent over forty years immersed in the history and philosophy of the social sciences and I say this without regret but great joy. Anthropology, sociology, philosophy, history, and psychology have constituted the focus of my interest and their relationship to the phenomenon of religious behavior has been the over-arching agenda in my research and writing. Individuals, dead and living, and institutions, far and near, have all contributed to this passion and facilitated my work. To name them all would seem excessive and, quite frankly, self-aggrandizing. But particular individuals must be named and specific institutions must be identified lest I appear too solitary in my own sense of self-worth.

My best friend in seminary was Foy Richie, now a pastor and psychotherapist himself, who introduced me to the great individuals about whom I have written in this book. He spoke with passion and insight about these persons of whom, at the time, I knew nothing at all. He did, and he challenged me to learn of them likewise. Leighton McCutcheon, my seminary psychology professor, chided me early for my assuming that the "concepts" of psychotherapy could be grasped without first learning the "terminology" of the psychotherapeutic traditions. Bhabagrahi Misra, my seminary anthropology professor at seminary, introduced me to Clifford Geertz and I was forever better for it. Robert Batchelder, my sociology professor at seminary, introduced me to Peter Berger and Karl Mannheim and my work has always been done within sight of their work. Richard Underwood, my philosophy professor at seminary, showed me that without a philosophical understanding of the history of ideas, my future academic career would be futile. Willem Bijlefeld, my history of religions professor at seminary, taught me that religio-phenomenology in the G. Vander Leeuw tradition would serve well my interest in understanding the experiential dynamic operative within every faith community. Rabbi Samuel Sandmel, my postdoctoral advisor at the Hebrew Union College Jewish Institute of Religion, showed me how being a leader of a faith community is an advantage rather than a disadvantage to provocative scholarship. Edward O. Wilson has had a major impact upon my work and my recent book on ethical naturalism I have, with his consent, dedicated it to him as an expression of my gratitude for his friendship. Robley Edward Whitson, my doctoral advisor and thesis supervisor, showed me how to do scholarship with passion as well as with empathy and critical assessment and with a spirit of fair play. Khutb Uddin is one of my closest friends, a member of my faculty at the Foundation in psychiatry, and has always and quietly inspired my interest in psychotherapy.

Besides these early teachers and current colleagues, there are places which made it all possible. I taught anthropology at the University of Connecticut, philosophy at the University of Hartford, psychology at the University of Texas, and sociology at Saint Mary's College of Notre Dame. I held postdoctoral appointments at Harvard, Yale, and Princeton and was three times a postdoctoral visiting scholar at the University of Chicago. Following an appointment at the University of Notre Dame as a National Science Foundation Science Faculty Fellow, I began teaching a summer doctoral-level seminar at Oxford University's theology program and was appointed to the Board of Studies there as well. Most recently, I have been made a member of the Advisory Board of the Centre for Religion and Public Life at Oxford University and for these appointments and many other kindnesses shown me by my friends and colleagues at Oxford, I am deeply grateful and particularly to Vincent Strudwick, Angus Hawkins, Robin Gibbons, Jane Shaw, Tom and Barbara Tinsley, Christopher Day, Liza Denny, and the late John Macquarrie. Their friendship has made the joy of my time at Oxford immense.

TABLE OF CONTENTS

INTRODUCTION 9
A Statement about Methodology and Terminology
Chapter I.............................21
    Sigmund Freud and Psychoanalysis (1856-1939)
Chapter II 51
    Alfred Adler and Individual Psychology (1870-1937)
Chapter III 75
    Carl Gustav Jung and Analytical Psychology (1875-1961)
Chapter IV............................95
    Viktor Frankl and Logotherapy (1905-1997)
Chapter V...........................113
    Abraham Maslow and Humanistic Psychology (1908-1970)
Chapter VI..........................133
    Erik Erikson and Developmental Psychology (1902-1994)
Chapter VII.........................155
    Carl Rogers and Person-Centered Psychotherapy
    (1902-1987)
Chapter VIII........................179
    Harry Stack Sullivan and Interpersonal Psychoanalysis
    (1892-1949)
CONCLUSION..............................195
GLOSSARY OF TERMS.................197
BIBLIOGRAPHY.........................217
ABOUT THE AUTHOR...................229
INDEX...................................231
EDITORIAL NOTE

For ease of reading, I have chosen to use the masculine pronoun form throughout owing both to the cumbersomeness of using he/she and to respect the classic texts being quoted in this study, all of which were products of their weltanschauung and, therefore, used the masculine form as generic to humankind.

INTRODUCTION

Believing that the use of primary sources is the best way of learning the thought system of a great thinker, I have decided to focus upon a single text of each of the eight psychotherapists considered in this book. Though the entire corpus of their work will be incorporated in this enquiry, our approach will be to critically consider a major text which established each one as a leading theorist in the field of psychotherapy. We will provide a biographical summary of each theorist followed by a textual analysis of a classic work in their repertoire. We will also include a comprehensive bibliography of each theorist and a glossary of terms relevant to each system of psychotherapy considered here. This work can be criticized for not incorporating all of each theorist's writings but for two reasons, that will not be done. First, their literary output makes that impracticable, and, second, a carefully considered treatment of one classic text seems preferable to a cursory glance at their entire literary corpus. Finally, we will consider the fundamentals of their thought in relationship to the practice of psychotherapy. Following the biographical sketch there will be an in-depth consideration of a primary text in the published *repertoire* of the eight psychotherapists being considered here. This author is convinced that nothing can substitute for acquaintance with the primary source of a thinker, no matter how good the secondary source is, for the reading of the original thinker must always trump the reading of one who has thought about the original thinker! Then and finally, we will explicate a few key concepts and theories for closer examination.

This three-step process, i.e., biography, major text, key concepts and theories, I believe provides an easy to manage approach to both an introduction and a summary overview of each system of thought. By approaching the materials in this fashion, the uninitiated will have a quick and systematic exposure to the theorists and their theories and the already initiated veteran will enjoy an easy to use guide to that which they are already familiar. Thus, both the uninitiated and the veteran might benefit from our efforts here to present in a systematic fashion the life and work of eight major psychotherapists in the 20th century.

Presently, there are over one thousand titles in print which claim, at various levels of authenticity and scholarship, to be an introduction to the thought of some, if not all, of the psychotherapists and psychologists we are about to discuss. Our intention here is not to simply duplicate that awesome array of intellect and redundancy. My intention, rather, is to be of some assistance to a community of professionals with whom I have had the privilege of associating for some fifty years or so, namely, pastors involved at various levels of ministry in offering counseling to the troubled, disturbed, and worried members of society. Pastoral counselors are a breed unto themselves as they come in all flavors, from the highly trained post-ordination psychotherapist touting credentials of advanced learning in the field to the lowly parish pastor who made it through divinity school to ordination and little more. My compassion is for both and all those in between. Pastors involved in counseling, whether depth analysis or triage, have my sympathy, first, because few in their faith community understand their training and even fewer understand the pressures of the profession.

So, I have taken in hand as one with years of experience in working with such pastors to put together a ready summary of the best of the best in psychotherapeutic theory. That is to say, I have determined to offer a refresher course in "The Classical Tradition of Psychotherapy" specifically for the busy pastor who would greatly treasure and even benefit from such a summary. I propose no new insights into psychotherapy. Rather, I propose to put in one little text a compilation of all of the great thoughts and theories of those who have been responsible for, blamed, and credited for having developed psychotherapeutic modalities of treatment valuable for use by pastors in the parish setting.

Naturally and understandably, everyone will not be happy with the selection I have made here of the "classical" tradition. No one, I think, will fault the ones I have chosen but many will fault me for not having added more. And, indeed, I could have added more. I could have added two, four, six, eight, even ten more and still some will not be completely happy with the roster of those treated in this little text. Yet, the ones chosen cannot be faulted for they have all earned their place in the history of behavioral science. The ones chosen are indisputably worthy of treatment and over the years I have taught a doctoral-level summer seminar at Oxford University dealing precisely with those considered here.

Let me simply say that I have chosen eight psychologists whose work has been particularly relevant to pastoral counselors as classical representatives of contemporary psychotherapy. From the birth of Freud in 1856 to the death of Frankl in 1997, the nearly one hundred and fifty years covered during that time period saw the rise and development of eight major theorists and eight major systems of psychotherapy to be discussed here. The Europeans, radiating out from Vienna, include Freud, Jung, Adler, Frankl, and Erikson, and the Americans considered here are Sullivan, Maslow, and Rogers. The Viennese school did not really include either Carl Gustav Jung or Erik H. Erikson. However, Jung did begin with Freud in Vienna and became somewhat famous because he broke with Freud in Vienna. He, of course, practiced and built a world reputation from Zurich, and we are all aware of that. Erikson's involvement in Vienna and his election at thirty-one years old to Freud's inner circle set Erikson on his way as a future player in the developmental psychology which eventuated in his high profile in America. For the Americans, there are many more which could have been included. I lost little sleep, however, in including the four I chose because no one in the profession of applied psychology or psychotherapeutic counseling would find fault with the ones' chosen. So, I have chosen the safe path, namely, include everyone that everyone would include and exclude those whom some would have chosen but other would have excluded.

If we can learn anything from this summary text, then my work will have been justified. If we only have our memories jogged to recall the classic theories of the classic thinkers, I feel my time would not have been wasted. The worst that can happen, then, is that the reader will simply say, "I knew that already," to which I might reply, "Good, I thought you might." Not wishing to add anything "new" but simply to remind professionals of what we already know about the various schools of psychotherapy will do me must fine, and my publisher seems to be happy with the agenda as well. As my grandmother used to say to me, "It doesn't hurt to be reminded of what you already know!" And, with that mandate, I have undertaken to remind my professional colleagues of what they already know.

Of course, before we can consider the concept of "psychotherapy" and its great theorists, we need at least to acknowledge the breadth and depth of "personality theory" as a major enterprise within the discipline of psychology. Not every theorists in the field of psychology is pleased to begin, or even end, their work with this concept but those theorists being considered in this enquiry have most certainly commenced their work here. Early the last century, G. W. Allport of Harvard had already gleaned over fifty operational definitions of personality, and in the subsequent generations, a plethora more have been generated. We need not review them all here! Rather, we will focus upon several "categories" of personality theories which more or less have relevance to our own specific agenda here. We will briefly summarize "Trait theories," "Psychodynamic and psycho- analytic theories," "behaviorism," "Social learning theories," "Situationism," and "Interactionism," and will draw par- ticularly from Arthur S. Reber's thorough treatment in his now classic *Dictionary of Psychology* published by Penguin.

All theories of the "trait" variety operate from the assumption that one's personality is a compendium of "traits" or "characteristic ways of behaving, thinking, feeling, and reacting." The early trait theories were actually little more than lists of adjectives and personality was defined simply by enumeration. More recent approaches have used techniques of factor analysis in an attempt to isolate underlying dimensions of personality. Probably the most influential theory here is that of R. B. Cattell, which is based on a set of "source traits" that are assumed to exist in relative amounts in each individual and are the "real structural influences underlying personality." According to Cattell, the goal of personality theory is to have the individual trait matrix formulated so that behavioral predictions can be made. It should be noted that the "type" and "trait" approaches complement each other and, indeed, one could argue that they are two sides of the same coin. Type theories are primarily concerned with that which is common among individuals, trait theories focus on that which differentiates them. However, they certainly entail very different connotations of the base term "personality."

A multitude of approaches is clustered here as psychodynamic and psychoanalytic theories including the classic theories of Freud and Jung, the social psychological theories of Adler, Fromm, Sullivan and Horney, and the more recent approaches of Laing and Perls, to mention only a few key theorists. The distinctions between them are legion but all contain an important common core idea: namely, personality for all is characterized by the notion of "integration." Strong emphasis is generally placed upon developmental factors, with the implicit assumption that the adult personality evolves gradually over time, depending on the manner in which the integration of factors develops. Moreover, motivational concepts are of considerable importance, so that no account of personality is considered to be theoretically useful without an evaluation of the underlying motivational syndromes.

The focus in behaviorism has been on the extension of learning theory to the study of personality. Although there are no coherent, purely behaviorist theories of personality, the orientation has stimulated other theorists to look closely at an integral problem: how much of the behavioral consistency that most people display is due to underlying personality "types" or "traits" or "dynamics" and how much is due to consistencies in the environment and in the contingencies of reinforcement? Not surprisingly, the points of view below, all of which were influenced to some degree by behaviorism, look beyond the person for answers here and, to some degree or another, actually question the usefulness of the term "personality" altogether.

Much of the theorizing from the point of view of social learning theories derives from the problem just outlined. However, the notion of personality is treated here as those aspects of behavior that are acquired in a social context. The leading theorist here is Albert Bandura, whose position is based on the assumption that although learning is critical, factors other than simple stimulus-response associations and reinforcement contingencies are needed to explain the development of complex social behaviors (such as "roles") that essentially make up one's personality. In particular, cognitive factors such as memory, retention processes and self-regulatory processes are important and much research has focused on modeling and observational learning as mechanisms that can give a theoretically satisfying description of the regularities of behavior in social contexts.

The perspective of "situationism," championed by Walter Mischel, is derivative of the preceding two positions. It argues that whatever consistency of behavior is observable is largely determined by the characteristics of the "situation" rather than by any internal personality types or traits. Indeed, the very notion of a personality trait, from this point of view, is nothing more than a mental construction of an observer who is trying to make some sense of the behavior of others and exists only in the mind of the beholder. The regularity of behavior is attributed to similarities in the situations one tends to find oneself in rather than to internal regularities.

The position of "interactionism" is a kind of eclectic one. It admits of certain truths in all of the above, more single-minded, theories and maintains that personality emerges from interactions between particular qualities and predispositions and the manner in which the environment influences the ways in which these qualities and behavioral tendencies are displayed. It is far from clear that personality can be said to exist as a distinct "thing" from this perspective. Rather, it becomes a kind of cover term for the complex patterns of interaction.

It is interesting to note that the above theoretical approaches can be seen as representing two distinguishable generalizations concerning the very term "personality." For the categories of traits theory and psychodynamic and psychoanalytic theories, it represents a legitimate theoretical construct, a hypothetical, internal "entity" with a causal role in behavior and, from a theoretical point of view, with genuine explanatory power. For behaviorism, social learning theories, situationism, and interactionism, it is seen as a secondary factor inferred on the basis of consistency of behavior — while other operations and processes play the critical causal roles in dictating behavior — and, hence, as a notion that has relatively little explanatory power.

What is Psychotherapy? The answer to this question is easy and it is not; it is simple and it is certainly complex. Before we can fairly commence a summary of the classical schools of psychotherapy, it might be fair to offer a working definition of this field of health care practice and to suggest the perimeters of its value and function. At the end of this little study, we will offer an Appendix of terms relevant to the practice and theory of psychotherapy. Beyond that, we will attempt here to offer a brief definition of the practice of psychotherapy which pastors and counselors can easily identify with for professional practice.

Thanks to the generosity of Arthur S. Reber and the publishers of the *Dictionary of Psychology*, by Penguin Books, we have ready access to "the" authoritative definition. Of course, we will not be hamstrung by this definition, we will simply commence here. Reber says, "In the most inclusive sense, the use of absolutely any technique or procedure that has palliative or curative effects upon any mental, emotional or behavioral disorder can be called "psychotherapy." In this general sense of the term is neutral with regard to the theory that may underlie it, the actual procedures and techniques entailed or the form and duration of the treatment. There may, however, be legal and professional issues involved in the actual practice of what is called psychotherapy, and in the technical literature the term is properly used only when it is carried out by someone with recognized training and using accepted techniques. ... the term is often used in shortened form, therapy, particularly when modifiers are appended to identify the form of therapy or the theoretical orientation of the therapist using it.

Psychotherapy is, as a professional practice, an interpersonal and relational "intervention" used by trained professionals in the treatment of clients who are experiencing difficulty in daily life. The focus is usually upon issues related to "well-being" and the attempt to reduce personal senses of dissatisfaction with one's life. Practitioners of psychotherapy use a wide variety of techniques devised by theorists in the field dealing with problematic issues of life's daily functions. Such simple things as improving dialogue skills, communication development, and behavioral modi- fication are employed in such treatment. The goal is the improvement and enhancement of mental health on the part of the client/patient.

Though contemporary practices in psychotherapeutic counseling have reached far beyond its early modality of treatment which, by and large, was limited to a "conversational" style of patient/client/counselor relationship, to include today such modes of interaction as writing, artistic expression, drama, therapeutic touch and even aroma therapy, we will limit ourselves to the classic mode of encounter, viz., conversation. This structured and highly orchestrated therapeutic encounter between therapist and client/patient dates from the earliest beginnings of psychotherapy in the late 19th century. Whereas once psychotherapy was thought to be limited to behavioral crises and counseling to the more mundane behavioral adjustments needed for a well-directed life, that line of distinction has all but vanished these days with "psychotherapy" being used as both the term for and practice of intensive counseling encounters. Yet, where as counseling has not frequently been thought of in terms of the medical model, interventionist psychotherapy is most commonly so characterized. Again, however, given the rise of clinical pastoral education which is most commonly practiced and taught in a medical setting, even that line of distinction has vanished more or less.

These variances in terminology and usage have created something of a problematic situation for pastors who both wish to be trained in and to offer psychotherapeutic counseling to their pastoral constituencies and yet wish to avoid any appearance of treading on the medical profession's rightful domain. The use of such terms as counselor, therapist, client, patient, clinical, etc. has often created ambiguities in the minds of both the practitioner and the recipient. There is no set rule though some have tried to establish them. There are, however, state laws affecting the use of such terms as counselor and psychologist which pastoral counselors would be wise to explore before launching out into this cauldron of psycho-medical and psycho-clinical practice. Let us agree here early on that we will use "psychotherapy" and its variants to apply to pastoral counseling, and we will use the term "client" rather than "patient" to refer to the recipient of such psychotherapy. For pastoral counselors preferring to use the term "counselor" to describe what they do, we will honor that and, also, for psychotherapist who prefer to consider the recipients of their professional skills "patients" rather than clients, we will honor that position as well. For our purposes, however, we will say psychotherapist when referring to pastoral counselors and clients when referring to their patients.

Needless to say, since the time of Sigmund Freud, without doubt the father of modern psychoanalysis, there have emerged several rather distinctly identifiable systems or schools of psychotherapy. We will not consider any of these in detail except as they might relate to the "classical" traditions to be considered here later. As we know, Freud was a trained medical neurologist and was early on interested in the seemingly non-biogenic behavioral disorders and this interest led him to develop and utilize such analytical techniques as dream interpretation, free association, the concept of transference, and the tripartite id/ego/superego construct of the human psyche. Regardless of one's own ideological bias or professional training today, few would dispute the fact that Freud is the Father of the Movement known as psychoanalysis and its contingent, psychotherapy. Under the broader concept of "psychodynamics," many schools of thought were spawned by Freud's pioneering work with some staying close to his theoretical moorings as neo-Freudians while others moved far a field as post-Freudians. However, all schools of psychodynamics engaged in psychotherapeutic application addressed themselves necessarily and inevitably to the whole concept of the psyche's conscious/subconscious/unconscious reality.

Of course, not all psychologists and those engaged in the behavioral sciences chose to use Freud as a launching pad. The behaviorism of B. F. Skinner and others evolved a "behavioral therapy" which has become quite popular in certain circles which uses such concepts as operant conditioning, classical conditioning, and social learning theory. And, eventually, such ideological positions as existential philosophy came into play in the development of certain schools of psychotherapeutic treatment such as Viktor Frankl's logotherapy. Extending existentialism was the work of Carl Rogers and Abraham Maslow whom we will consider in detail later. Their work, of course, lead to the rather popular "person-centered" school of psychotherapy and from that came Fritz Perls' gestalt therapy and Eric Berne's Transactional Analysis, all falling into a rather lumpy collection of what is passionately labeled humanistic psychotherapy today. Other and diminishingly important schools of thought were spawned by this rash of post-Freudian and even post-Satrean existentialists thought into such things as cognitive therapy following Aaron Beck, and postmodernist trends known as narrative therapy, coherence therapy, transpersonal psychology, feminist therapy (as a separate school of its own!), somatic psychology, expressive therapy and, for want of a better descriptive term, brief therapy.

Most of these, of course, we will discard for our discussion of what I am insisting upon calling the "classical schools of psychotherapy," which, as we have already stated will consist only of four members of the Viennese schools of psychoanalytic psychotherapy (including the Jungian variant) and the American schools of psychotherapy. The two schools, then are limited to, in the first instance, Freud, Adler, Jung, and Frankl and in the second instance, Maslow, Erikson, Rogers, and Sullivan. For ease of cross referencing, I will refer to the first school as the Viennese Schools and the later as the American Schools. I have already defended my right to include Carl Gustav Jung in the Viennese Schools even though he formally launched his analytical psychology school in Zurich after having left Freud and Adler in Vienna. Yet, without Freud and Vienna, there would arguably be no Jung. Whether I am right or wrong, I will stay with this operational perspective for, if no other reason, ease of reference.

Vienna is unquestionably the original city of psychotherapeutic psychology. The city produced Freud, Adler, and Frankl, founders of the three great schools of Viennese psychotherapy. Jung, who fell under the sway of Freud and worked closely with Adler, hailed, however, from Zurich, but we consider him in this group owing to the influence upon his developing thought of those early Viennese years. Nevertheless,

Vienna is the First City of depth psychology and it all began with Freud. Of course, before Freud there was psychology and before either there was Vienna. Vienna was, for centuries and without dispute, the center of European life and culture as the convergence point of East meeting West. Being located on the Danube river and just under the Austrian Alps, it was quite naturally a key trading center. For over five hundred years, the Hapsburgs had ruled there and under the care and nurture of the incomparable Maria Theresa and Joseph II in the late 1700s it gained an international reputation as the center of western music, producing such composers as Haydn, Mozart, Beethoven, and Schubert.

Jews and other religious and ethnic communities, however, found little to revel in under the Austro-Hungarian Empire, certainly until the revolution of 1848 when everything changed. Emperor Franz Joseph, for example in 1849, introduced a constitutional law mandating that "civil and political rights are not dependent on religion." Now, the Jews and other oppressed groups could breathe, for the moment, a breath of fresh air of freedom, including the opening of wider options in career choices and the ownership of real estate. By 1867 when a new constitution was adopted for the Austro-Hungarian people, Jews were even being elected to the Vienna City Council even while the Empire was constitutionally Christian. Because of this liberalism, the Jewish population of Vienna grew from 6,000 in 1860 to 150,000 in 1900 creating the largest Jewish population in Western Europe. Though racial and religious prejudices still thrived, to be sure, Vienna was a relative safe haven for aspiring Jews and it is at this point that we pick up our story of the development of psychoanalysis and the psychotherapeutic schools developed by the Jewish medical community under the separate but collaborative convergence of Freud, Adler, and Frankl.

Chapter I

Sigmund Freud
and Psychoanalysis

BIOGRAPHICAL SKETCH

"Psychoanalysis is the sickness of which it claims to be the cure" say the critical pundits of Freudian psychoanalysis. Though he began in a cloud of professional suspicion, every professional today practicing in the cognate fields of counseling are beholden to Freud and his system of theory and analysis whether they will admit it or not. But to admit being beholden does not mean that one is bound to it. Gratitude has its place, however, and we will see in the following discussion the range of Freud's work as exemplified in his life, theoretical development, and analytical methodology. Whether one comes away from this discussion convinced or confused, for or against, it is our intention to make sure that upon leaving Freud and his system of psychoanalysis that the reader has a clearer idea of what there is to believe or disbelieve about it in its own terms. One can only be critical of that which one fully and clearly understands. We aim here, then, for clarity of vision and then, and only then, will we have a right to say "yeah" or "neigh" to Freud and his followers.

To be fair to the development of any theory, and some might suggest this is particularly true of psychological theory, there is the need to understand the theorist. By this we mean, know from whence he came, who he was, what he did, and, as best we can, grasp his own self-understanding of his life and work. So let's take a look or, if the case may be, another look at the life of Sigmund (Sigismund) Freud, a 19th century physician from Vienna. We will review his life, his theories, and then take a close look at his classic, *Civilization and Its Discontents.*

Freud's parents were practicing Jews and though he denied the existence of God, believing such a belief was essentially a neurotic dependence as a substitute for emotional maturity, he did very much prize his Jewish tradition and culture. His father, Jakob Freud, was from a region in southeastern Europe consisting of a large minority of Jews called Galacia. He was a wool merchant and following the 1867 Emancipation of the Jews in the Austrian Empire and his marriage and the birth of their first son, Sigmund, the Freuds moved first to Leipzig and then to Vienna where Sigmund Freud would live the next eight years. Jakob had done what many ambitious Jews were doing, namely, he embraced a reasonable compromise between his Jewish culture and the business and secular culture around him. Though it has been suggested that he was secretly a closet Hassid, Jews who embraced a kind of mystical tradition based on the sacred book called the Kabbala, he was able to effect an integration into Austrian secular culture without relinquishing his Jewish faith. His mother, Amalia Nathanson, was from a distinguished and well-to-do Jewish family of Galacia. She was Jakob's second wife for he had two sons, approximately her own age, at the time of their marriage. Over the next ten years of marriage, Amalia gave birth to eight children, the first being Sigmund on May 6, 1956. She was acclaimed to have been very attractive, authoritarian, and a great admirer of his first born son, Sigmund. Though born in Freiburg, Moravia (now Pribor in the Czeck Republic), Freud at the age of four moved with his family to Vienna where he would live, except for the final fifteen months of his life living in London, for the next eighty years.

Without doubt, Freud was precocious, a mama's boy, and an excellent student in the schools of Vienna. It is said that his retentive visual memory and exceptional writing skills elevated him to the highest levels in school and, even though he was uncertain as to his career goals, he was early on predisposed to biology and was greatly influenced during his formative years by the evolutionary theory of Charles Darwin whose monumental work was published in 1859. In Vienna, Freud attended the Leopoldstadter Kommunal-Realgymnasium, a prominent high school, and Freud proved most outstanding, graduating the "Matura" in 1873 with honors. Eventually, Freud first considered studying law, which was now permitted to Jews, but finally entered medical school at the University of Vienna in 1873 which was under the direction of the famous Darwinist Professor Karl Claus. In no particular hurry, he completed his medical degree in eight years which allowed him an addition three years beyond the five year minimum for medical degrees to expand his interests in philosophy and literature. From research in zoology and comparative anatomy during his medical school years, Freud shifted his interests and activities to microanatomy, becoming the lab assistant to the distinguished Viennese Professor Ernst Brucke who, though a positivist, influenced Freud considerably in the areas of physics and chemistry. A German physiologist, Professor Ernst Wilhelm von Brucke, in collaboration with Professor Hermann von Helmholtz, were proponents of the use of the concept of "psychodynamics" in the study of living organisms. In 1874, this concept was radical and revolutionary and Brucke and Holmholtz explicated the theory in the publication of their studies entitled, *Lectures on Physiology*. Any living organism, of special interest being the human person, is a dynamic system to which the laws of chemistry and physics apply. This, it should be pointed out, is believed to be the beginning of Freud's dynamic psychology of the mind and his concept of the unconscious.

During these crucial formative years, Freud was greatly influenced by a postdoctoral fellow, Dr. Joseph Breuer, who worked in Brucke's laboratory and shared with Freud details of various cases of hysteria including the now famous case of Anna

O. Following a mandatory year in military in 1879, Freud returned to work in Brucke's lab after finishing his medical exams during which time he translated a book by John Stuart Mill dealing with empiricism. Though very much disinclined to practice medicine, Freud had fallen in love with Martha Bernays, an attractive and strong-willed Jewish girl from a very distinguished Viennese family. In fact, Martha's grandfather was Isaac Bernays, chief rabbi in Hamburg. The road to financial solvency was through the practice of medicine and that was a requirement to gain permission to marry. So, Freud resigned himself to practice medicine and the specialization he chose was clinical neurology. Due to his having distinguished himself as a teaching assistant at the medical school, he was taken on staff at the highly prestigious Viennese General Hospital. Having tried hypnosis in his private practice, he was dissatisfied with the results and turned to what he eventually came to call simply the "talking cure" in the treatment of mental disorders.

During the following few years at the VGH, he engaged in various research projects including work on the use and effects of cocaine as a stimulant, an aphrodisiac, and a cure for morphine addiction which was quite common at the time due to medical practices in service hospitals. Unfortunately, he came under increasing scrutiny and criticism due to his work in the area of addiction and a major paper he wrote on the use of cocaine in opthamological surgery fell on deaf ears at the local medical association meetings. He subsequently passed in his examination to become a *privatdozent* (private lecturer) at the University of Vienna in the field of neuropathology and following his official appointment was given a traveling grant to study with the famous psychologist and neurologist of Paris, Jean Martin Charcot. Freud always attributed this experience to his turning from traditional neurophysiology towards the practice of medical psychotherapy.

Two major experiences served Freud's long term interest in treating mental disorders. First, Charcot demonstrated how non-hysterical patients could be trained under hypnosis to exhibit hysterical symptoms such as paralysis and tremors, and second, Charcot demonstrated how physical symptoms of hysteria were derived from mental activity, thus, hysteria seemed clearly to be a "mental" disorder rather than merely a biogenic malfunction. Ironically, it was Charcot who first suggested to Freud the importance of sex by indicating that frequently sexual problems were related to mental disorder, particularly hysteria. Alas, whereas Freud went to Paris to become a neurologist, he returned as a fledgling psychiatrist!

Co-authoring with his old lab colleague, Dr. Josef Breuer, Freud drew more attention to himself with the publication of their 1895 highly acclaimed *Studies in Hysteria* which, according to historians of psychology, marks the actual beginning of psychoanalysis as a school of thought. Freud's chapter on psychotherapy established him as a major voice in this new field. Though deeply committed to his relationship with Breuer, Freud began a long and tedious journey away from his old colleague owing to Freud's heavy emphasis upon the essential role assigned to sex in the etiology of all neuroses. Breuer's tentative hesitation gave rise to a deepening gulf between them and finally resulted in a permanent break. This friendship was replaced by William Fliess, an ear, nose, and throat surgeon from Berlin who for the next several years proved to be Freud's closest confidant in the gradual development of the theories of psychoanalysis.

As is common knowledge, the fundamental bases of Freud's development of psychoanalytic theory grew out of his own self-analysis. Confidence in himself ran high and low but overall Freud continued to believe in himself and his ability to develop therapeutic modalities which would facilitate his capacity to plumb the depths of his own psyche, particularly his unconscious through, initially, the interpretation of dreams. On the strength of his insights into mental functions gained from his practice as a psychiatrist, he gradually and unequivocally developed a psychosexual theory of personality development that would dominate psychoanalytic theory for the next hundred years.

His confidence is reflected in a statement made in correspondence to his friend and colleague, William Fliess, when he wrote: "I cannot give you an idea of the intellectual beauty of the work."

Freud became convinced over a period of years of intense self-analysis that dreams are essentially disguised forms of infantile wishes and thought processes and the meanings of them can be discovered by means of the analytical modalities developed in psychoanalysis, particularly dream analysis. In 1900, he published what has been recognized by most practitioners as his most distinguished book, *The Interpretation of Dreams.* The publication of this book marked the end of his emotionally wrenching self-analysis and the beginning of his drive to establish psychoanalysis as the dominant school of psychotherapy. He was now free to move beyond his old confidants of bygone days, namely, Charcot, Breuer, Brucke, and Flliess. He would no longer look to them for counsel nor seek from them advice in his future work. Psychoanalysis was his creation and it was his place to establish it throughout the western world as the undisputed leading school of psychotherapy.

Needless to say, Freud was not revered nor loved by many of his professional colleagues. Freud was a Jew, a self-promoting johnny-come-lately who proposed to plumb the depths of the human psyche using unorthodox methods and non-clinically tested and proven techniques boarding on the scandalous. That a self-respecting physician and psychiatrist would propose to foist off on the unsuspecting public hocus-pocus spells designed to interpret mentally disturbed patients' dreams was more than many could take and they let it be known throughout Vienna that Freud was to be watched. The criticisms were in print and on the tongues of many respected physicians and psychiatrists of the day and, therefore, Freud had his work cut out for himself and his new school of psychotherapy called psychoanalysis. His two books to-date didn't help much as they were hardly read until years after he had become a household name and respected internationally.

Yet, among the medical establishment there were brave and inquisitive physicians eager to learn more and to be engaged in this new adventure. Five key practitioners proved early on most helpful and though all but one eventually abandoned ship, while they were involved they proved most reassuring to Freud and his fledgling organization called the International Congress of Psychoanalysis held for the first time in 1908. The next year saw the launching of the journal which proved pivotal in the stabilizing of the movement. The five key figures were Karl Abraham of Germany, Carl Jung of Switzerland, Ernest Jones of Great Britain, and Alfred Adler and Otto Rank of Austria.

Psychoanalysis was destined to become the American craze for the new and different. To facilitate that unwittingly, the president of Clark University in Massachusetts, an ambitious new institution seeking to make a name for itself, invited Freud, among others, to come to America to participate in the celebration of the University's twentieth anniversary. G. Stanley Hall, the President of the University, was America's leading psychologist at the time, a position shared with William James of Harvard, and Hall had been known to say of Freud and psychoanalysis that it was "a series of fads or crazes." Yet, invite Freud he did and come Freud did, giving five outstanding, though unprepared, lectures on psychoanalysis. Later, these essays were prepared for publication back in Vienna and went a long way in advancing the case for psychoanalysis in Europe and most especially in America.

However, as the professional organization of psychoanalysis began to grow by leaps and bounds, bringing on more and more young psychiatrists in Europe and especially in America, the seasoned veterans of the early formative years began to resist and counter theoretical developments within psychoanalysis which were approved by Freud but not by the old guard. Alfred Adler broke with the orthodox school over issues related to the dominance of sex-based theorizing, preferring to focus upon the human drive to mastery or "the will to power" whereas Carl Jung, who was designated the heir-apparent by Freud himself, moved with precision and strategy to establish his own school of thought, called "analytical psychology." These were major blows to the professional organization and only with sustained focus upon the orthodox theories did Freud and his followers weather the storm of dissent without permanent damage. These other schools of thought will be discussed later.

In the midst of it all, Freud never stopped treating patients. For a physician who early and publicly proclaimed a distaste for the profession, Freud practiced nearly sixty years as a physician. During that time he concentrated upon fine tuning his theories, exploring new territory, and developing new insights in mental illness. He published extensively and prolifically, both in book form and periodicals. Three major works beyond those first two already mentioned were *The Psychopathology of Everyday Life* (1901), *Introductory Lectures on Psycho-analysis* (1916-1917), and *New Introductory Lectures on Psycho-analysis* (1933). One never to be accused of not continuing to press forward with investigations, analyses, and theoretical explorations, Freud moved beyond just an interest in the individual patient to broader social issues of the day. Both social psychology and social philosophy became a sustained interest of his during his waning years of productivity and his now highly acclaimed classic, *Civilization and Its Discontents* represents him at his best. It is an application of psychoanalytic theory to the broad social issues of human behavior in society. This study of Freud's, written when he was in his closing years of life, offers a pessimistic view of the human condition. The best life has to offer is merely a compromise between the inevitable and the irreconcilable demands that dominate our existence. The year he published this now famous work, 1930, was the year the German government awarded him the Goethe Prize in appreciation for his contribution to psychology and to German literary culture. It is this book we have chosen to study more systematically later in this chapter.

The very personal and tragic side to Freud's life has to do with both the necessity of his leaving his home in Vienna and the physical struggles with his health. When Freud turned sixty-six years old, he was diagnosed with mouth cancer brought on, it was believed, by his addiction to cigars. Over the next nearly twenty years he underwent thirty operations including the removal of the entire roof of his mouth which was replaced by a metal prosthesis which he called "the monster." Yet, he continued to write and see patients through it all. In 1938, Vienna saw the annexation of Austria to the German Reich by Adolph Hitler, bringing with it the oppression of the Jews without discrimination or regard for professional status in the community.

With much insistence from his professional colleagues and friends who knew that both Einstein's physics and Freud's psychoanalysis were anathama to the Nazi, Freud with his wife and youngest daughter Anna fled to London where he died fifteen months later. Freud prevailed upon his personal physician and friend, Dr. Max Schur, to assist him in taking his own life. At this time, Freud wrote to Schur: "My dear Schur, you certainly remember our first talk. You promised me then not to forsake me when my time comes. Now it is nothing but torture and makes no sense any more." Schur administered three doses of morphine over many hours that resulted in Freud's death on September 23, 1939. The pain of the final stages of Freud's cancer led him to this decision. Freud's body was cremated in England during a service attended by many Austrian refugees and his ashes were placed in the columbarium there at Golders Green Crematorium where his wife, Martha, was likewise buried in 1951 and later his daughter Anna as well. His four younger sisters, now in their old age, were murdered in the SS concentration camps of Germany. To those who rejected his theories, Freud is said to have responded to G. Stanley Hall: "They may abuse my doctrines by day, but I am sure they dream of them by night."

THE CLASSIC TEXT CONSIDERED

The primary text to be considered here was published by Freud in 1930 in Vienna under the title, *Das Unbehagen in der Kulture,* and simultaneously in London in translation, *Civilization and Its Discontents.* All references here will be taken from the College Edition newly translated from the German and edited by James Strachey and published by W. W. Norton and Company of New York in 1962.

This little classic of Freud's will be reviewed for its address to and perspective upon the meaning of human life (a theme we will hold up throughout this study), especially as conceived in the context of human development which inevitably counter-poses the principle of pleasure with the principle of reality. Here, we will find Freud saying, "...the purpose of life is simply the programme of the pleasure principle," and since the human person is unable (for personal reasons) or not permitted (for social reasons) to gratify his desire for pleasure, he must learn that "satisfaction is obtained from illusions..." The tensions resulting from the desire for pleasurable gratification on the one hand and the encounter with social reality on the other hand make for a life-experience characterized by anxiety and neurosis which are most readily coped with through illusions. Therefore, in a real sense, says Freud, "...or civilization is largely responsible for our misery...:" What then can the meaning of life be? This is the question Freud pursues here.

The impact that Freud's thought has had upon Western culture in the last century is profound. Since the publishing of his *DIE TRAUMDENTUNG, 1900 (THE INTERPRETATION OF DREAMS,* 1955), Freud's thought has gained such widespread usage that it would be difficult to imagine a modern world devoid of his contributions to the understanding of the individual in society. If his studies of the human psyche have revolutionized our thoughts about and attitudes toward the unconscious, his writings on religion, society, and culture have shaken older images of human experiences and ushered in a new era of religious and social theorizing.

Not unaware of the profound shock his thought would have on modern times, Freud saw himself in a select line of great minds who have shaken the Western World. There have been three narcissistic shocks to Western consciousness, thought Freud. First was the Copernican or Cosmological shock which shook Western culture loose from his anthropogeocentric cosmology which located humanity and the earth at the center of the universe. This rude awakening brought trauma to Western thinkers who then had to learn how to live in a world where neither the human person nor the earth could claim centrality, but rather had been pre-empted by a heleocentric cosmology. The sun, a gaseous ball devoid of life, became the center.

The second and equally traumatic shock to the Western mind was dealt by Charles Darwin – the Biological Shock – which demonstrated the biological relatedness of all living things, humanity included. If Copernicus had challenged the status of humankind in the universe, Darwin had surely succeeded in establishing the dependence of humanity upon the earth and our kinship with all earth's creatures. The fact that we had persisted even after Copernicus in an anthropocentrism which over-valued the differences between us and animals as well as between various genetic groupings within the human family made even more difficult the acceptance of Darwin's revelation. To this very day, there are vocal if not large pockets of supposedly modern people who still decry the atheism erroneously assumed implicit in Darwin's biology and still lay claim to a primitive worldview nurtured by a creation-story literalism.

Last and most profound of the shocks to Western consciousness has been the Psychological Shock mercilessly dealt by Sigmund Freud. The shock was ushered in by a succession of scientific bomb-blasts: *THE INTERPRETATION OF DREAMS (1911), TOTEM AND TABOO (1912), BEYOND THE PLEASURE PRINCIPLE (1920), THE FUTURE OF AN*

ILLUSION (1927), and CIVILIZATION AND ITS DISCONTENTS (1930). By no means the whole bibliography of profound, challenging, and highly controversial studies, these works are exemplary of the breadth of Freud's research and interests. His study of the origin and function of religion, published under the significantly descriptive title, *THE FUTURE OF AN ILLUSION*, is without question his most controversial and most widely read study outside the specific field of psychoanalysis. And yet, his *CIVILIZATION AND ITS DISCONTENTS*, which reviews the arguments in the religion book, represents his most mature thoughts on human society and the individual's relation to it. David Bakan, in his provocative and highly controversial study on Freud, entitled, *SIGMUND FREUD AND THE JEWISH MYSTICAL TRADITION (1969)*, has cogently argued that Freud was himself a most exemplary thinker in the Kabbalistic tradition of Jewish mysticism. Kabbalism was an esoteric tradition which chose for reasons of safety and privacy to speak of the human spiritual condition in terms of the dark mysteries and primitive symbolisms of sexuality. If Bakan is right in this bit of theorizing, then the following statement from Freud gains even more profound eminence in modern religious thought: "The tendency on the part of civilization to restrict sexual life is no less clear than its other tendency to expand the cultural unit." But let us look more closely at his work before we pass judgment on Freud's either apt or warped view of the human condition.

The opening remarks in this brief statement of Freud's under scrutiny here are in reference to a friend who, though he entirely agreed with Freud's analysis of religion in his 1927 study, was concerned to call himself religious on the basis of a "sensation of eternity" or "oceanic feeling." Not only was Freud disinclined to accept his friend's suggestion, but Freud also wished to demonstrate how his feeling of eternity corroborated the ego-development schema of psychoanalysis.

The emergence of the ego ("...there is nothing of which we are more certain than the feeling of ourself, of our own ego (p.

12),'") says Freud, is "through a process of development...(p. 13)."
The ego is developmentally the inevitable result of a confronting
of the pristine libidinal impulses of the undifferentiated id with
the external world of sheer actuality. The id, having its
motivational impetus centered in the *pleasure-principle*, confronts
the *reality-principle* as the individual infant begins to discover
the unpleasantness of the otherness, separateness, and outsideness
of the real world. There is a strong motivation on the part of the
id-driven child to "separate from the ego everything that can
become a source of such unpleasure, to throw it outside and to
create a pure pleasure-ego which is confronted by a strange and
threatening 'outside' (p. 14)." The id begins necessarily to
develop a negotiating capability – the ego as executor of libidinal
powers — whereby the desires of the id are pacified with
substitute gratifications which are physically accessible and
socially acceptable. "In this way," says Freud, "one makes the
first step towards the introduction of the reality principle which
is to dominate future development (p. 14)."

Freud is here explaining a scenario of ego-development which
will address the issue of the oceanic feeling, and thus the subject
of religion. This executive function of the differentiated ego
serves as the primary medium of negotiation between the
pleasurable desires from within (the raw libido of the id) and the
realities of the outside world (social restraints upon behavior).
The more responsible the ego is to the reality-principle, the greater
the experience of separateness from the external world – "Our
present ego-feeling is, therefore, only a shrunken residue of a
much more inclusive, indeed, an all-embracing feeling, which
corresponded to a more intimate bond between the ego and the
world about it (p. 15)." There, Freud concludes that to the extent
that this earlier primary ego feeling of virtual nondifferentiation
of self and world in infancy has persisted alongside the narrower
demarcated ego feeling of self separate from the world in maturity,
there is the likelihood that feelings of "limitlessness and of a
bond with the universe," i.e., the oceanic feeling, will be present.

Freud contends that "...in mental life nothing which has once been formed can perish...(p. 16)," and, therefore, such feelings as these considered here are simply the residue of infantile experience. And though Freud is reluctant to connect the feeling of "oneness with the universe" with the origins of religion, he is "perfectly willing to acknowledge that the 'oceanic' feeling exists in many people, and (is) inclined to trace it back to an early phase of ego-feeling." In conclusion to this topic of oceanic feelings, Freud is wont to trace the origins of the oceanic feeling to "a first attempt at a religious consolation," which is to say, a feeling resulting from the developing ego's growing awareness of the external world. Furthermore, he is anxious to rearticulate his 1927 theory of religious origins, which says that "The derivation of religious needs from the infant's helplessness and the longing for the father aroused by it...(is) incontrovertible, especially since the feeling is not simply prolonged from childhood days, but is permanently sustained by fear of the superior power of Fate (p. 16)." Though this point will be considered in a later context, it must be noted here that for Freud, the energy output demonstrated by the ego's undying efforts to responsibly direct the otherwise unbridled powers of the id is the result of a deep feeling whose function is the "expression of a strong need." The religious feeling, says Freud, is a source of energy because it is expressive of a powerful need, viz., the helpless infant's longing for a powerful father.

In considering religion, Freud consistently was "concerned much less with the deepest sources of the religious feeling than with what the common man understands by his religion...(p. 2)." And yet, he was often so convincing in his critique of religion's object being nothing more than an "enormously exalted father" that it is difficult if not impossible to separate the "deepest" from the "common" in religion. Freud had no patience with the "great majority of mortals" who were infantilely dependent on this projected father-image as a substitute for ego-development and personal maturity. "The whole thing is so patently infantile," complained Freud, a painful reality that most people, avoiding true maturity, opt for a "pitiful rearguard" attachment to childish fantasies of a loving Providence which, watching over us, will reward us eternally in heaven if we are good.

The question of "the purpose of human life," says Freud, bespeaks humanity's "presumptuousness." Religion alone can answer this question, for the whole "idea of life having a purpose stands and falls with the religious system (p. 23)." And though these metaphysical complexities lie outside Freud's investigation here, he chooses to get at the question by an inquiry into the nature of human behavior which demonstrates humanity's purpose and intention in life. And in answer to this question, "What do men show by their behavior to be the purpose and intention of life?", Freud answers simply, "They strive after happiness, they want to become happy and to remain so." That is, they seek the "absence of pain and unpleasure" while seeking the "experiencing of strong feelings of pleasure." Therefore, Freud concludes, the rhetoric of religion to the contrary notwithstanding, "what decides the purpose of life is simply the programme of the pleasure principle."

Happiness, i.e., the satisfaction of needs too seldom gratified, is difficult to realize and impossible to sustain. Society is ever ready to condemn violations of its laws, and unrestrained self-gratification, i.e., personal happiness, inevitably results in a clash of the individual's desires (pleasure principle) and society's rules (reality principle). Therefore, "unhappiness is much less difficult to experience" because the individual is threatened with suffering from three sides: from our own body due to its finitude, from the external world with all its rules, and from our relations with other people. Since happiness is hardly possible at all, and never for any significant duration, we have necessarily had to develop techniques for controlling the instincts which given free rein would inevitably bring catastrophe to the individual and to society.

Through the executive services of the ego, the libidinal forces are displaced (focused upon a secondary and socially acceptable object choice) and the instincts are systematically sublimated. In the movement from pleasure to reality, the individual adopts two kinds of "satisfaction...obtained from illusion...(which arise out of) the imagination (p. 27)." Both religion and the enjoyment of the arts are the result of sublimated instincts and displaced libido. Freud says:

> A special importance attaches to the case in which this attempt to procure a certainty in happiness and a protection against suffering through a delusional remoulding of reality is made by a considerable number of people in common. The religions of mankind must be classed among the mass-delusions of this kind. No one, needless to say, who shares a delusion ever recognized it as such. (28).

And, says Freud, those who define happiness in life as the pursuit and love of beauty fail to realize that aesthetic impluse is simply the result of an ungratified primary sexual motivation. The tensions experienced in the perpetual struggle between the desire for happiness (pleasure principle) and avoidance of pain (reality principle) often lead to neurosis and even psychosis. "Any attempt at rebellion (against society, i.e., reality) is seen (either) as psychosis," or "as a last technique of living, which will at least bring him substitutive satisfaction, (i.e.)...that of a flight into neurotic illness." Freud's concluding remark regarding the function of religion in this context is worth quoting:

> Religion restricts this play of choice and adaptation, since it imposes equally on everyone its own path to the requisition of happiness and protection from suffering. Its technique consists in depressing the value of life and distorting the picture of the real world in a delusional manner
> – which presupposes an intimidation of the intelligence.

At this price, by forcibly fixing them in a state of psychical infantilism and by drawing them into a mass-delusion, religion succeeds in sparing many people an individual neurosis. But hardly anything more. (Pp. 31-32).

Why has humankind singularly, collectively, and consistently failed in our quest for happiness and the prevention of suffering? In attempting to answer this question, Freud says that a kind of "suspicion dawns on us" which says that maybe the answer lies in "a piece of our own psychical constitution." That is, the contention which "holds that what we call our civilization is largely responsible for our misery...(for) it is a certain fact that all the things with which we seek to protect ourselves against the threats that emanate from the sources of suffering are part of that very civilization (p. 33)."

Can it be? Civilization serves both to protect us against nature and to adjust our mutual relations. Wherein lies the evil, then? Certainly our civilization bore the culture from which came technical skills, fire and tool usage, writing and dwelling houses. And also, we invented gods to whom were attributed our own cultural ideals. Furthermore, beauty, cleanliness and order became "requirements for civilization." And of all characteristics of civilization esteemed and encouraged most highly are our higher mental activities, i.e., intellectual, scientific and artistic achievements, and "foremost among those ideas are the religious systems." The "motive force of all human activities," argues Freud, "is a striving towards the two confluent goals of utility and a yield of pleasure...(p. 41)."

The last and significantly problematic characteristic of civilization is the manner in which relationships of individuals to one another are regulated, i.e., family and state. "Human life in common," contends Freud, "is only made possible when a majority comes together which is stronger than any separate individual and which remains united against all separate individuals." Thus, a concept of the right or social good develops in opposition to individual brute force. "This replacement of the power of the individual by the power of a community constitutes the decisive step in civilization (p. 42)." The first requirement of this newly formed community is, therefore, justice – the assurance that the good of the many expressed in law will be honored over the desires of any single individual. "The liberty of the individual is no gift of civilization." And in this connection, Freud would have us see that there is a great "similarity between the process of civilization and the libidinal development of the individual." As sublimation functions in the individual for the development of a strong ego and creative capacity to deal with the principle of reality, so likewise, "sublimation of instinct is an especially conspicuous feature of cultural development; it is what makes it possible for higher psychical activities, scientific, artistic or ideological, to play such an important part in civilized life (p. 44)."

As we move closer to Freud's perception of the nature of the individual in society – our stumbling futile attempts to construct a viable meaning to life – we are confronted by an indispensable dialectic between life and death, especially as Freud had earlier developed the idea in his book, *BEYOND THE PLEASURE PRINCIPLE (1920)*. He explains its development:

> There still remained in me a kind of con-viction...that the instincts could not all be of the same kind...Starting from speculations on the beginning of life and from biological parallels, I drew the conclusion that, besides the instinct to preserve living substance and to join it into ever larger units, there must exist another, contrary instinct seeking to dissolve those units and to bring them back to their primordial, inorganic state. That is to say, as well as Eros there was an instinct of death (p. 66).

Within every society, as within every individual, there are

two conflicting instincts. The life instinct is at the service of
society so long as society is devoid of aggression, for aggression
is a stark manifestation of the Death instinct. Aggression, says
Freud, "is an original, self-subsisting instinctual disposition of
man...(and it) constitutes the greatest impediment to civilization."
Eros and Death share "world-dominion" and explain the
movement of civilization back and forth upon the scale of
creativity and destruction. This eternal and unexplainable struggle
is essentially what life is all about, and the evolution of civilization
is simply described "as the struggle for life of the human species."
There is only futility in attempting to explain the meaning of life
beyond this simple reality – the meaning of life is the struggle of
life against death. "And it is this battle of the giants," concludes
Freud, "that our nurse-maids try to appease with their lullabies
about Heaven (p. 69)."

It is the super-ego which constitutes the source of the human
feelings of guilt. The super-ego evolves in consort with the
development of the ego. As the ego gains relative control over
the id, it does so by means of taking to itself the moral expectations
of society, as society in turn, through the agency of parents,
impresses its values upon the child. The super-ego is the projection
of society's self-image into such an exalted state as to elicit
devotion and adoration. But as the ego becomes educated to the
reality principle, as a balancing source to the id's pleasure
principle, the super-ego is being socially reinforced in the adoption
of an ideal principle. As the ego's sense of reality confronts the
super-ego's sense of the social ideal, tension results within the
individual. The super-ego serves as the conscience which testifies
against the ego's reluctance to support the ideals of society. "The
tension between the harsh super-ego and the ego that is subjected
to it," says Freud, "is called by us the sense of guilt; it expresses
itself as a need for punishment (p. 70)." The stronger the ego,
the weaker the super-ego, and vice versa. Society's moral
expectations are mediated through the child's parents and give
rise to a conscience educated to certain idealistic expectations.

"Civilization, therefore," says Freud, "obtains mastery over the individual's dangerous desire for aggression by weakening and disarming it and by setting up an agency within him to watch over it..."

Guilt, which is really a social anxiety though frequently misnamed "bad conscience," often results from a "fear of loss of love" on the one hand and a "fear of punishment" on the other. But fundamentally, our sense of guilt springs from the Oedipus complex "which was acquired at the killing of the father by the brothers banded together" as classically illustrated in Freud's scenario of the development of primeval human community in his *TOTEM AND TABOO* (1912). And thus, what began in relation to the father is completed in relation to the group. Freud reasons:

> If civilization is a necessary course of develop-ment from the family to humanity as a whole, then – as a result of the inborn conflict arising from ambivalence, of the eternal struggle between the trends of love and death – there is inextricably bound up with it an increase of the sense of guilt, which will perhaps reach heights that the individual finds hard to tolerate (p. 80).

It was Freud's intention from the beginning "to represent the sense of guilt as the most important problem in the development of civilization and to show that the price we pay for our advance in civilization is a loss of happiness through the heightening of the sense of guilt (p. 81)."

Quick to make a qualitative distinction between a "sense of guilt" and a "consciousness of guilt," Freud argues that guilt plays its greatest role in the human experience when operating in the unconscious. And when functioning here, "...the sense of guilt is at bottom nothing else but a topographical variety of anxiety; in its later phases it coincides completely with *fear of the super-ego* (p. 82)." To the extent that guilt remains unobserved in the dark chambers of the unconscious, we are condemned to writhe in our own dissatisfaction – a sort of *malaise* produced by civilization itself. "Religions," says Freud, "have never overlooked the part played in civilization by a sense of guilt." The sense of guilt, the harshness of the superego, the severity of the conscience – all are demonstrative of a need for punishment. This need, says Freud, "is an instinctive (manifestation on the part of the ego) which has become masochistic under the influence of a sadistic super-ego..." Religion, as an illusion produced out of the imaginations of sublimated instincts, functions as a social neurosis which protects us from the stark realities of life devoid of any ultimate transcendent meaning. Mature individuals must eventually rid themselves of illusion and imagination and learn to face squarely and without guilt the meaninglessness of life.

Freud's attitude towards life's meaning is capsulated in a quotation from his study, *CIVILIZATION AND ITS DISCONTENTS*, with which we conclude our discussion:

> The fateful question for the human species seems to me to be whether and to what extent their cultural development will succeed in mastering the disturbance of their communal life by the human instinct of aggression and self-destruction...

One thing only do I know for certain and that is that man's judgments of value follow directly his wishes for happiness – that, accordingly, they are an attempt to support his illusions with arguments. (P. 92)

THEORIES AND CONCEPTS

Unless we begin with Freud, we cannot proceed with any degree of insightfulness regarding the rise of modern day psychotherapeutic practice. That there are a myriad of psychotherapeutic modalities employed daily in hospitals, clinics, counseling centers, and residential treatment facilities goes without saying. But that the proliferation of these various and sometimes competing modalities of treatment is the outgrowth of Freud is indisputable. We have chosen in this study to focus upon eight schools of thought and we have continued to insist that given their originality they all owe homage, even if ever so grudgingly given, to the birth of psychoanalysis.

Sigmund Freud has established himself as the instigator of one of the three Cosmic Shocks to western culture. Whereas Copernicus shocked the intellectual world by demolishing the notion that man is the center of the universe (the Cosmological Shock) and Darwin with his discovering of the emergent evolution of life on this plant (the Biological Shock), Freud presented to the modern world an insightful discovery of the nature and role of the unconscious in our daily lives (the Psychological Shock). Modern science and the understanding of humanity will never be the same due to these three great discoveries. And so, without reason dissent, we must begin with Freud who, during his forty years of psychoanalytic practice, developed the first comprehensive theory of personality, developed a thoroughgoing method of treating mental illness, and produced an extensive body of clinical literature based upon his theories and methods of treatment.

In the following, we will look at four areas of Freud's work which have the greatest impact upon counseling practice today, and they are (1) levels of consciousness — conscious, preconscious, unconscious, (2) psychosexual development, (3) the structure of personality, and (4) psychoanalytic therapy. The intent is not to produce a comprehensive survey of Freud's work but to present the four major categories of his work which have an immediacy and relevance to the practice of counseling in the modern setting.

In Freud's fascination with and desire to describe the functioning of the human mind, he set out to develop a map of how the human mind worked. He was intrigued with the possibility, even the necessity, of delving into the inner workings of the human mind to understand the relationship between the function of the mind and human behavior and he came to believe that much of what goes on in human behavior is cued by the human mind in ways unknown to and not understood by the conscious person. He was, essentially, committed to a "psycho-cartography" of human behavior, a "mapping of mind function." In this process, he believed he had discovered that the human mind consists of three levels of function —the conscious, the preconscious, and the unconscious. To understand the nature of human behavior, the therapist must understand the interrelationship of these three levels, how they affect each other, and how to accept their content for closer scrutiny for only by doing so can the therapist understand the "why" of behavior.

The conscious level of the human mind includes everything that the individual is aware of at any given moment. This, of course, includes thoughts, perceptions, feelings, memories, etc., but really constitutes only a small part of mental functioning. Freud believed that a "selective screening process" functioned to permit only certain information to be at any given moment immediately available to the mind and he was interested in why this screening process was necessary and what it excluded from immediate awareness of the conscious person.

The preconscious (or what is now more commonly called "subconscious") dimension of the human mind consists, said Freud, of all that which is available to memory but is not populate immediate awareness but requires an intentional reflection but is free from the "screening" process of the unconscious. Freud believed that the subconscious functioning of the human mind constituted a sort of link between conscious and unconscious. Most if not all of what is in the subconscious domain of mental function is available, upon demand, by the conscious functioning of the individual but, when that information is no longer needed in the immediacy of living, falls back into the subconscious compartment of the human mind.

It is to the unconscious reservoir of the human mind that Freud was most attracted because it is here, he believed, that much of what affects human behavior resides but subject to the screening function of the conscious mind. Though certainly not the first western thinker to ponder the unconscious mind, Freud was decidedly different in his queries from the 17th and 18th century philosophers who speculated about the complex functioning of the human mind because Freud brought both a medical and an empirical commitment and insight into his investigations. The unconscious was, for Freud, not merely a "hypothetical abstraction" to be pondered and wondered at, but rather was an empirically functioning part of the human mind. To understand the unconscious functioning of the human mind would provide real insight into human behavior, especially and particularly mental illness.

As a physician and psychiatrist, Freud was deter-mined to plumb the depths of that compartment of the human mind which, while radically affecting human behavior, seemed ever to elude consciousness and the human will's capacity to control it. Because unconscious components of the human mind are inaccessible to the conscious mind, given the conscious mind's intent upon protecting itself from the materials found in the unconscious compartments of the mind, it was Freud's belief that a psychologically-driven archaeology of the mind would release this screened information which affects human behavior. By releasing or exposing of this material, the patient suffering from mental illness caused by this protected material (later called repressed material) could commence a journey towards mental health. The screening and protecting mechanisms of the conscious mind for this unconscious material include dreams and fantasies, and it was here that Freud set about to do his work and, eventually, to develop what he called "psychoanalysis."

Within the context of this psychocartography of the human mind, Freud believed that the human personality was comprised of three fundamental structures which worked in consort with the three levels of consciousness. These three personality constructs he called the "id," the "ego," and the "superego." Believing that these personality constructs were essentially "hypothetical" as are the three constructs of consciousness, due to the insufficiently of microanatomy to locate them within the central nervous system, he nevertheless insisted upon their reality and their primary functioning within the human mind and the human personality. Whereas the id functions within the domain of the unconscious, the ego is primarily located in the preconscious or subconscious and conscious portions of mental functioning with the superego superimposed over the domain of the ego with capabilities of affecting the functions even of the unconscious domain of mental processes.

The id, Freud believed, was the repository of all instinctual functions of the human animal and is governed by the "pleasure principle" which we have discussed earlier. It is essentially uninhibited and irrational and functions strictly under the energy of animal drives, particularly sex and aggression, and is the cause of tension within the person owing to a confliction of instinct and control. To understand the relationship between the driving energy of the id and the mandated social comportment and propriety of the ego would go a long way in identifying the causes of human stress and resulting mental illness. The maturation process of the human animal, then, is directly related to the process of mediating between instinct and social order, between the demands of the id and behavior deemed appropriate by the ego.

The ego, then, is that part of the personality which seems to pacify the irrational desires of the instinctual id while guiding behavior to appropriately moderated forms of acceptable behavior. The stronger the ego, the more controlled the person is in terms of social expectations of propriety; the weaker the ego, the less control and, thus, the greater the danger of violating the rules of society. It is the ego which is responsible for the protection and survival of the individual for the id is only interested in immediate gratification without regard to safety or propriety. Whereas the id is governed by the pleasure principle, the ego is governed by the reality principle. Primary process governs the id because instincts are dominant; secondary process governs the ego because reason and logic take the upper hand. Finally, we can say that the ego is the "executive branch" of the human personality and the center of intellect and propriety.

While the ego is the executive branch of the personality, moderating the demands of the id while honoring the propriety of the ego, it is to the superego that the personality must go for guidance regarding appropriate behavior. The ego is moderator but not the instigator of the individual's sense of values, norms, and attitudes. These fall to the domain of the superego. If the superego is extremely restrictive and controlling by providing only a short rope for existential decision-making, then the ego is repressed in its capacity to be creative. A repressed ego results in a warped and dysfunctional personality due to the lack of creative spontaneity for the ego to manage the id. The superego is an "outside" force, introduced in the maturation process of the human individual. It is the mother, the parents, the community, society at large and the world of religion which constitute the source of the superego. With the coming of issues related to good and bad, right and wrong, we see the emergence of the superego. Balancing the irrational demands of the id with the social demands of the superego is the responsibility of the ego and the ego develops in direct relationship to the capacity to manage the tensions produced by this balancing function. Herein lies the fertile ground for mental illness brought on by stress and anxiety.

The superego consists of two countervailing forces — the conscience and the ego-ideal. The conscience is concerned with compliance to parental and social demands about right and wrong, good and bad, behavior. Whereas the conscience has to do with guilt-inducing non-compliance, the ego-ideal is derived from approved behavior of parents and society. The aim is for self-control to replace parental control, but whereas the id is controlled by instincts and is based on the pleasure principle, the superego is controlled by socially approved behavior and is based on the reality principle as negotiated by the ego. The trouble comes when the superego presses beyond the reality principle to perfectionist goals beyond the capacity of the ego to respond. Much psychiatric fall out from religious fanaticism is located in this complexity of interactive struggles between id, ego, and superego.

Complimenting Freud's concept of the three levels of mental functioning — conscious, subconscious, unconscious — is his notion of the four-stage sexual development of the human personality - oral, anal, phallic, and genital. It is quite evident that these stages are named for the specific regions of the body from which sexual energy is discharged. Each stage is identified, then, with what Freud called a "primary erogenous" zone. The term "psychosexual" emphasizes quite clearly his agenda in exploring these developmental stages and their functions in the development of human personality and, of course, their relationship to mental illness. Freud is emphatic about the nature and function of these development stages of human personality and paid a dear price throughout his career for his insistence upon their utility in analysis.

The *oral stage* characterizes the first year of life when the infant is fixated on oral gratification and its relationship to feeding. Though an important erogenous zone throughout life, the mouth is primary during the first year of life and sucking and tactile sensitivity around the lips is fundamental to the infant's development and ends at the time of weaning. Freud believed that in cases where either there was excessive or insufficient amounts of stimulation there is likely to emerge an oral-passive personality in adulthood, such a personality is characterized by having an optimistic view of the world, having established trusting dependent relationship with others, and one who expects others to "mother" him. This person's psychological adjustment is characterized by gullibility, passivity, and immaturity.

The *anal stage* comes during the second and third year of life and involves a shifting of the child's attention from the mouth to the anal region of the body, particularly retention and expulsion of feces and urine. The bowels and bladder become a major focus of attention in children of this age and depending upon the parental guidance in this area, the child is destined to a sound personality development or one severely warped by mismanagement. Freud believed that many cases of mental illness derived specifically from this stage in personality development. He was convinced that the way in which parents carry out toilet training has specific effects on later personality development and claimed that all later forms of self-control and mastery issues have their origin in the anal stage of development.

The *phallic stage* comes during the fourth year of development when the libidinal interests of the child shifts erogenous zones from the anus to the sex organs. Psychosexual development during this stage includes genital manipulation for pleasure, masterbation, and a growing verbal interest in matters related to birth and babies and similar topics usually posed to the parent. It is during this stage that Freud's now famous concept of the Oedipus complex emerges. The classic concept in Freudian psychoanalysis is used to indicate the situation where the child of either sex develops feelings of love and/or hostility for the parent. In the simple male Oedipus complex, the boy has incestuous feelings of love for the mother and hostility toward the father. The simple female Oedipus complex exists when the girl feels hostility for the mother and sexual love for the father. Psychoanalysts generally agree that adult males who fixate at the phallic stage are usually brash, vain, boastful, and ambitious. Phallic types strive to be successful and attempt at all times to assert their masculinity and virility. In the case of women, Freud believed that the phallic fixation results in traits of flirtatiousness, seductiveness, and promiscuity even though the individual may appear naïve and innocent in sexual relationships. He further believed that the primary source of subsequent neurotic patterns of behavior related to impotency and frigidity derive from this stage of personality development.

The *genital stage* comes with the onset of adolescence and puberty. Following what Freud called the latency period of relative calm, the pubescent child experiences an increased awareness of and interest in the opposite sex. Due to biochemical and physiological changes in the body, the child is now subjected to an influx of drives and desires heretofore unknown or unacknowledged. Freud believed that most children at this point go through a homosexual stage during which time the child, girl or boy, fixates on a same-sex friend or acquaintance. Eventually, the shift to the opposite sex usually occurs with the onslaught of "crushes" and "puppy love." Freud believed that for an adult to attain the ideal genital development, that person must relinquish the passivity of early childhood days when love, security, physical comfort, etc., were freely available and must learn to work, postpone gratification, become responsible, and above all, assume a more active role in dealing with life's problems.

Though we have explored in detail Freud's personal life and his work, looked at a major text of his, and here have reviewed a few of his monumental contributions to psychoanalytic theory, we should not leave until we have explored briefly the therapeutic practice of psychoanalysis as employed by Freud. As with all eight schools of psychotherapy we are considering here, the theoretical foundations have been built for the purpose of psychotherapy rather than merely an exercise in theory building. Freud was intent upon constructing a psychodynamic psychotherapy utilizing his conceptual insights into the nature of the human mind as it relates to mental illness and mental health.

Psychoanalytic psychotherapy has been developed for the purpose of addressing virtually all forms of mental illness. Freud was not reluctant to draw from a variety of social and behavioral sciences such as sociology and anthropology as well as both philosophy and religion in the development of his system. It was Freud's clinical experience of working with neurotic patients which generated his fundamental insights into mental illness and which led to the development of this monumental school of thought. It was upon the clinical experience he had as a practicing psychiatrist that he relied in the testing of his hypotheses. "The teachings of psychoanalysis," Freud said, "are based on an incalculable number of observations and experiences, and no one who has not repeated those observations upon himself and upon others is in a position to arrive at an independent judgment of it."

The fundamental "tools" of the psychoanalytic practitioner include Freud's well-developed concepts of free association, interpretation of resistance, dream analysis, and analysis of transference to probe the patient's unconscious with the aim of making possible a deeper understanding of self. These newly acquired self-insights are then converted into the person's everyday life through the method of emotional reeducation.

Chapter II

Alfred Adler
and Individual Psychology

BIOGRAPHICAL SKETCH

What we have said about Freud's Vienna can likewise be said of Adler's Vienna as they were essentially contemporaries (Freud 1856-1939; Adler 1870-1937). And, they were both Jews and eventually physicians and psychotherapists. Adler's father, Leopold was born in 1835 in the Burgenland but at the time Leopold married Adler's mother, Pauline Beer, in 1866, they became residence of Pauline's hometown. The Beers were Czechoslovakian Jews from Moravia, not unlike Freud's family, and were by the time of the marriage of Leopold and Pauline successful business people operating the firm of Hermann Beer and Sons, dealing in bran, oats, and wheat. The first child of this marriage of Leopold and Pauline was Sigmund (1868) followed two years later by Alfred, born February 7, 1870, in the village of Rudolfsheim, a near suburb of Vienna.

These were happy days for Adler as he says: "As far as I can look back, I was always surrounded by friends and comrades, and for the most part, I was a well-loved playmate. This development began early and has never ceased. It is probably this feeling of solidarity with others that my understanding of the need for cooperation arose, a motive which has become the key to Individual Psychology." His outgoing and gregarious personality and the ease with which he made new friends he himself traced back to this blissful days of youth. Yet and alas, he failed to maintain such friendship into adulthood.

The preference shown Adler's older brother, Sigmund, and the unhappy death and circumstances of Adler's little brother Rudolf both conspired, in his mind, to rouse an interest in medicine. Never religious and no identifiable interest in the religious side of Judaism, the Adlers deemed Judaism an encumbrance to their progress in society. Yet, little Alfred did find the Biblical stories a source of insight into human nature not unlike Freud's use of the Kabbala. Living in Leopoldstadt, the most Jewish district of Vienna, the Adlers were imbedded in the Jewish culture from dawn to dusk throughout Alfred's childhood and adolescence. Being an eager assimilationist, Alfred Adler would eventually converted to Protestantism, with little regrets to hear him tell it.

Adler's pursuit of a medical career was indicative of the aspirations of many modern Jews of the time. Dominated by his older and more outstanding brother, Adler later would suggest that he was, to use a formalized term later in his theories, "compensating" for physical weakness by achieving success in the profession of medicine. In the spring of 1888, he graduated from the Hernals *Gymnasium* and, at the age of eighteen, he was accepted into the University of Vienna's school of medicine. He completed the entire course of study in seven years, average for the time, taking only the minimum courses and examinations and passing with the lowest possible grades from the medical school and, interestingly enough, received no training in psychiatry.

Because of Adler's parentage, he held Hungarian citizenship and, therefore, in Austria the only medical experience available to him was working as a volunteer medical worker in the Viennese Poliklinik, a free medical hospital for working-class families. During these years of service and growing out of the experience in the public hospital, Adler became an enthusiastic socialist and became a member of the Social Democratic Party. Because of the financial success of his older brother, Sigmund, the entire Adler clan lived better than most during these economically and politically troubling years.

In 1897, everything changed for Alder because he fell in love for the first, and only, time in his life. She was Raissa Timofeivna Epstein. Alder never spoke nor wrote about how they met and the history of the relationship was forever veiled in mystery. She was born in Moscow in 1873 into an affluent Jewish family. Her mother died when Raissa was very young and her childhood was not happy. She attended the University of Zurich, the University of Moscow barring women from attending, studying biology, zoology, and aiming for a degree in the natural sciences.

At aged twenty-seven and twenty-four respectively, Adler and Raissa were married on December 23, 1897, with a full compliment of families on both sides in attendance in the city of Smolensk, Russia. Though she desperately missed her large family after the wedding when they returned to Vienna to Alder's medical practice, she gave birth the following year to their first child, Valentine Dina. In the meantime, Adler's medical practice and reputation were growing by leaps and bounds and he was already working on some theories of his own which included such formalized terms as organ inferiority, compensation, and overcompensation. These will be considered more formally later in this discussion

At twenty-eight years of age, Adler published his first in what would be a long series of scholarship articles. It was a short monograph entitled, *Health Book for the Tailor Trade*, and reflected his passion for the working-class medical conditions, a concern which would characterize his entire professional career. During these years, domestic tranquility seemed to elude them as Adler had virtually no contact, by choice, with his two sisters and two brothers, and Raissa likewise had little family interaction. Yet, Adler's career continued to thrive and he continued to publish right along. Adler naturally came in contact with Freud as they both practiced medicine and psychiatry in Vienna and the history and complexity of that on-again off-again relationship we will only mention in passing later. Suffice it to say here that, at Freud's personal invitation, Adler was asked to join Freud's Wednesday Psychological Society as the youngest member of this small group of young psychiatrists and physicians.

In 1904, Adler published the most important article of his young career, an article that would set the stage for his climb to fame in Europe and America and a topic which would characterize the duration of his professional career. It appeared in *Aertzliche Standeszeitung*, entitled, "The Physician as Educator," with the overriding emphasis being upon the physician's role as "preventer" rather than "curer" of illness among children with special attention to their psychological health. That same year and without his wife, Alder and his daughters converted to Protestantism. Not an unusual occurrence at all among Jews of his status in Vienna, he was a nominal Christian at best but they all celebrated Christmas enthusiastically. And, another bridged crossed and burned was the break with Freud, a long and tedious and never-to-be-clearly understood topic. Adler relied upon the "drive for assertion" rather than Freud's emphasis upon "sexual gratification" and, thus, since both were strong willed and strong minded, they broke at the same time Carl Jung was leaving as well (more later on this). To counter Freud's Vienna Psychoanalytic Society, Adler founded in Vienna his own independent Society for Free Psychoanalytic Study. The break was clean and final and issued in the most productive period of Adler's professional life.

His domestic life seems to have settled down quietly and the recollections of his adult children confirm that impression. Emphatically opposed to physical punishment, both Adlers chose to explore deprivation as a punishment rather than hitting. All the while, he worked on with his analytical psychology, the Society publishing a new monograph series and him publishing his most important book to-date, namely, *Ueber den nervosen Charakter*, in 1912 and simultaneously in the United States as

The Neurotic Constitution. Two years later, his colleagues launched with him their own journal, the *Journal for Individual Psychology* which set in motion the development of a whole school of psychotherapy called "Individual Psychology," all to the anger and hostility of Freud and his followers.

With the coming of World War I and the raging hostilities between Russia and the Austro-Hungarian Empire, the landscape seemed bleak in Europe and, naturally, individual psychology as a movement began to languish. In 1915 and after waiting for years for the appointment, Alder was finally being considered for an appointment as a Lecturer (without stipend) to the University of Vienna School of Medicine. But, where Freud had enjoyed for years a professorial appointment there, Adler was finally rejected even for this lowly honor. Because Europe (and it seemed the entire world) was falling apart with strife and hostilities, Adler argued that what was needed was "not more individualism" but what he called more "social feeling" (Gemeinschaftsgefuhl), meaning more compassion, altruism, and selflessness. He argued that social feeling was the infrastructural support of his newly developed individual psychology. In this notion, he was strongly supported by the American William Alanson White who became a colleague of Harry Stack Sullivan (of whom more in a later chapter). What struck a common cord with White and later Sullivan was Adler's contention that psychiatric disorders offered new evidence that "behind every neurosis is the existence of a weakling whose incapacity for adapting himself to the ideas of the majority calls forth an aggressive attitude taking on a neurotic form." This was particularly true of soldiers returning from the front lines of battle. At the war's end, some 15,000,000 soldiers and civilians had died in Europe and the face of western culture would forever be changed because of the carnage.

Following the war, there was a strong and growing movement towards Socialism, and Adler found himself in the very midst of the activity. Arguing eloquently that "capitalism is inherently inequitable in the distribution of goods and services," he would eventually embrace a political position which suggests that socialism is the moral barometer of capitalism. However, Adler never embraced the use of violence by the Communists to gain their goals, saying, "Human nature generally answers external coercion with a counter-coercion. It seeks its satisfaction not in rewards for obedience and docility, but aims to prove that its own means of power are stronger ... When in the life of man or the history of mankind has such an attempt ever succeeded? ... No blessing comes from the use of power." Finally, in 1920, Adler published a major collection of essays designed to establish individual psychology as a school of thought within psychotherapy, entitled, *The Practice and Theory of Individual Psychology*. These twenty-eight essays did the job. Acclaimed throughout Europe and America, Individual Psychology came into its own, particularly in the field of child psychology.

Coming immediately on the heels of this major collection was the reestablishment, following the ravages of WWI, of the movement's periodical, called the *Journal for Individual Psychology*, in 1923 with an internationally distinguished board of editors including the renowned American psychology G. Stanley Hall of Clark University. Yet and still, Individual Psychology as a school of thought, not unlike psychoanalysis of the Freudian camp, came under severe criticism from certain quarters. First, Adler and Adlerians were criticized for their casual if not indifferent attitude to statistics and their use in assessments and evaluations of treatment and counseling results, particularly as relates to children. Furthermore, this school of thought seldom if ever provided a systematic follow-up of their interventions when dealing with psychological problems of children and youth thereby leaving them open to criticism for failing to actually demonstrate effectiveness. Also, Adler's personal indifference to experimental work would eventually haunt him throughout the remaining years of his practice. Finally, Adler's inordinate emphasis upon environmental factors with a disregard to inherited behavior proved extremely problematic to establishing this school of thought as a major player in 20th psychotherapy. His naively employed motto when dealing with children of "Anyone can learn anything" made the movement seem thin and simplistic.

Yet, his involvement in child psychology and educational psychology did not go unnoticed in the wider profession. For example, in 1924 Adler was made professor of psychology with special interests in child developmental and educational psychology at the Pedagogical Institute's Division of Remedial Education. The Institute was a part of the University of Vienna and worked in consort with Karl and Charlotte Buhler's Institute of Psychology. But in America, Adler and Individual Psychology were becoming a major point of interest within both the professional community and the general public at large. Emphasizing the two fundamental principles of his theory, Adler was always quick to point out that "two factors affect all human relations, namely, the inferiority complex and the striving for social feeling. The New York Times described this "new psychology" of Adler this way: "One of the most important schools of this new science of the soul is individual psychology, founded by the Viennese scholar and neurologist, Dr. Alfred Adler. Laymen sometimes make the mistake of regarding individual psychology as a mere subdivision of the psychoanalysis of Freud. It is no more that than is Protestantism a subdivision of Catholicism." Such praise went far to establish Individual Psychology as a major player on the American stage.

In anticipation of and as a lead up to the publishing of his next major work translated into English in 1926 entitled, *Understanding Human Nature,* Adler gave a cryptic summary for the press of what he means by Individual Psychology. Individual Psychology regards the craving for power on the part of the individual and of nations as a reaction to deep feelings of inferiority. "Individual Psychology," he said, "could rally all the latent forces for good which are inherent in groups, just as it is already rallying such latent forces in individuals. Wars, national hatreds and class struggle — these greatest enemies of humankind — all root in the desire to escape, or compensate for, the crushing sense of their inferiority. Individual psychology, which can cure individuals of the evil effects of this sense of inferiority, might be developed into a powerful instrument for ridding nations and groups of the menace of their collective inferiority complex."

Adler's coming to America on the heels of this publication was fortuitously beneficial for his school of psychology. America was experiencing a major decline in religious attendance which was coupled with major upheavals in the social values related to marriage, romance, and sexuality. The popularity of the automobile was on the exponential rise as a portable living room for eating, drinking, smoking, gossiping, and sex. The liberation of American sexual mores centered in Hollywood and the coming of psychiatry and psychoanalysis as the new fads among the rich also served well the Adlerian agenda.

Freudian psychoanalysis, which was for a time the ruling school of thought among the top professionals and the wealthy in America, began to feel competition from Individual Psychology. Freud's anti-Americanism became increasing known and unwelcome as the lead up to McCarthyism. The radically subjective nature of his therapeutic treatment, its unending demand for weekly visits over many years, the overall expense, etc., all conspired to create an atmosphere of welcome for Alderian psychology as a radically different approach to mental health. Freud's criticism, first off the record then in later years on the record, of Americans as an uncouth, money-grubbing lot did not serve well his cause. Freud even went so far as to tell Ernest Jones, his famous biographer, that "America is a mistake; a gigantic mistake, it is true, but nonetheless a mistake." And, the fact that both Adler and Jung were experiencing a massive boost in their financial situations thanks to American interest grated hard on Freud and he didn't keep it to himself. A few clips from Freud's later statements about Americans and America will serve: "It often seems to me that analysis fits the American as a white shirt the raven." "What is the use of Americans if they bring no money?" "America is useful for nothing else but to supply money." "Is it not sad that we are materially dependent on these savages (Americans) who are not better-class human beings?"

America was ready for Adler thanks, ironically and in part, to the earlier arrival of Freud and psychoanalysis. Freud set the stage in America but Adler produced a more pragmatic approach to mental health. To professionals and the general public, Alder emphasized the concept of "inferiority" as a central theme to his understanding of human nature. "The behavior patter of persons," he would say in all of his lectures, "can be studied from their relation to three things: to society, to work, to sex. The feeling of inferiority affects a man's relations to these." Again, he said: "The three great questions in life that require answers by each individual have to do with occupation, society, and love. … (and the role of parents and teachers is to) help the child to create a style of life that is profitable for himself, for society, and for posterity." This was, indeed, well received in American audiences of professional counselors and teachers alike. His lecture series at the New School for Social Research in New York City in 1928 went a long way to further his reputation.

Adler never stopped emphasizing the need to stimulate in the child a sense of confidence, to evoke his cooperative dispositions, to socialize and humanize his ego, especially to teachers and parents. He was becoming the darling to the teaching profession and to educated parents concerned about the raising of their children in a "modern" world. In the *Saturday Review of Literature*, S. Daniel House of Columbia University wrote: "The Adlerian approach to the problems of disharmony and maladjustment resident in human nature constitute a new chapter in psychology and, what is more important, a fresh beginning in education…. We might refer to Adler's work as educational sociology and compare him in his general social philosophy and creative attitudes towards education with John Dewey. … he might be referred to with considerable accuracy as the pioneer in the comparatively new field of educational psychiatry."

Benefiting from such praise and desiring more and more to distance himself from both Freud and psycho-analysis, Adler spoke specifically to the issue In his lecture series at the New School for Social Research. In speaking of the differences, he said that "Freud takes as premise the fact that man is so constructed by nature that he wishes only to satisfy his drives but that culture or civilization is antagonistic to such satisfaction. However, Individual Psychology claims that the development of the individual, because of his bodily inadequacy and his feeling of inferiority, is dependent on society. Hence, social feeling is inherent in man and bound up with his identity." This did it for the American audience. Leading up to the occasion of him receiving an honorary doctorate from Wittenberg College in America, Adler said: "the most important single factor in personality development is the relative presence of the inferiority complex ... This feeling of inferiority forms the background for all our studies. It ultimately becomes the stimulus among all individuals, whether children or adults, to establish their actions in such a way that they will arrive at a goal of superiority." He subsequently learned that the Soviet Union had elected him an honorary member of the Leningrad Scientific-Medical Child Study Society, an accolade he was not willing to refuse.

Returning to America for the third time in 1929 to promote his latest book, *The Technique of Individual Psychology,* he continued to lecture at the New School on optimism and human nature to the delight of the professionals and students who flocked to hear him. That year, he made the decision to relocate permanently to America and New York, but without Raissa who was most disinclined to leave her European home and roots partly because of his increasing involvement in Austrian Communist Party activities. Alder, nevertheless, settled into his new residence, a suite at the Windermere Hotel on Manhattan's West End Avenue and Ninety-Second Street. The New York years saw his national reputation grow even while he continued relationships, mixed as they were, with the New School and Columbia University, taking a visiting professorships in medical psychology at the Long Island College of Medicine.

As the war mongering continued to accelerate in Europe leading up to the inevitable World War II, Adler was very concerned about his European family, none of whom were willing to consider coming to American in spite of his pleadings. Adler never returned to Austria following his last visit. At his leaving, he gave a book to a little boy who cared greatly for him. Adler later reported that as he left, the little boy ran down the road crying out to him: "Come back, and stay forever!" With this, Alder turned his back forever on Europe, save for a visit to England where he traveled with his wife, Raissa, for the last time. He returned to New York and continued to lecture, teach, and practice individual psychology until his death of a heart attack at the age of sixty-seven. Freud was reported to have rejoiced that he outlived Adler but many accolades from professional colleagues were published from such as Maslow, Rogers, and Frankl.

THE CLASSIC TEXT CONSIDERED

As Adler began to feel the power and strength of his own theory-building enterprise, he began, at first quietly and subtly but gradually both aggressively and outspokenly, to move away from Freud's fundamental argument that sexual conflicts in early childhood caused mental illness. Adler gradually began to consign sexuality to a symbolic role in human strivings to overcome feelings of inadequacy, what he came to call the inferiority complex. By 1911, Adler was speaking out loudly and publicly against Freud's funda-mentally erroneous mistake regarding the centrality of sexuality in child development. Adler and a group of colleagues eventually disassociated themselves from Freud and the classical psychoanalytic school of sexual dominance in mental illness and began the eventual development of what has become known as Individual Psychology, best and most thoroughly developed in Adler's 1927 book, *Menschen-kenntnis* (English translation, *Understanding Human Nature)*.

Without question, Adler's *Understanding Human Nature* (English translation by Walter Beran Wolfe) published and copyrighted in 1927 by the Greenburg Publishers of Garden City, NY, constitutes his most acclaimed work. We will review this book, commencing with excerpts from Adler's on Preface and followed by our review.

"This book is an attempt," wrote Adler, "to acquaint the general public with the fundamentals of Individual Psychology. At the same time it is a demonstration of the practical application of these principles to the conduct of one's everyday relationships, not only to the world, and to one's fellowmen, but also to the organization of one's personal life. ... The purpose of the book is to point out how the mistaken behavior of the individual affects the harmony of our social and communal life; further, to teach the individual to recognize his own mistakes, and finally, to show him how he may effect a harmonious adjustment to the communal life."

It is Adler's 1927 book, *Understanding Human Nature*, which captures our attention here for it was this book, more than any other, which commended his optimistic worldview and hopeful approach to the study of human development, especially of children, to America and the world. We will take excerpts from this great classic and our comments upon them we will place in italics.

We have often drawn attention to the fact that before we can judge a human being we must know the situation in which he grew up. *These are Adler's opening words when speaking of "The Family Constellation."* An important moment is the position which a child occupied in his family constellation. Frequently we can catalogue human beings according to this view point after we have gained sufficient expertness, and can recognize whether an individual is a first-born, an only child, the youngest child, or the life. *Adler was the first to place a major emphasis up what later became commonly called within psychotherapy "birth order" of the child. He was himself one of several and always felt confident that the order a child is born into the family would/ could/should have a major, and not always positive, impact upon his development. He spent a great deal of time researching and writing upon this factor even though, ironically enough, there is nothing anyone can do about the order of their birth in a family. His concern was for both the parents need to take full cognizance of the fact and to directly address that point in the childrearing practices employed in dealing with each child as well as the child, in adulthood, taking full cognizance of that reality as he reflects upon his childhood and how that reality may have affected his worldview.*

People seem to have known for a long time that the youngest child is usually a peculiar type. ... Not only is he the youngest, but also usually the smallest, and by consequence, the most in need of help. ... Hence there arise a number of characteristics which influence his attitude toward life in a remarkable way, and cause him to be a remarkable personality. ...One group of these youngest children excels every other member of the family ... But there is another more unfortunate group of these same youngest children ... which have a desire to excel, but lack the necessary activity and self-confidence, as a result of their relationships to their older brothers and sisters. *Adler was keen to place a great deal of emphasis upon the first child, the youngest child, and the only child as being of particular types and quite susceptible to both analysis and study as well as themselves being personally susceptible to certain psychological dysfunctions. As an educator as well as psychotherapist, he was especially concerned that full awareness of these realities be integrated into the educational system of the day.*

We are really tired of having nothing but the first and best people. History as well as experience demonstrates that happiness does not consist in being the first or best. To teach a child such a principle makes him one-sided; above all it robs him of his chance of being a good fellow man. The first consequence of such doctrines is that a child thinks only of himself and occupies himself in wondering whether someone will overtake him. Envy and hate of his fellows and anxiety for his own position, develop in his soul. His very place in life makes a speeder, trying to beat out all others, of the youngest. ... This type of the youngest child is occasionally to be found as a clear-cut type example, although variations are common. ... Another type, which grows secondarily from the first, is often found. When a youngest child of this type loses his courage he becomes the most arrant coward that we can well imagine. We find him far from the front, every labor seems too much for him, and he becomes a veritable "alibi artist" who attempts nothing useful, but spends his whole energy wasting time. ... He will always find excuses for his failures. He may contend that he was too weak or petted, or that his brothers and sisters did not allow him to develop. *Adler wishes to call attention to these two types of "youngest" personality options, the high achiever at any price and the low achiever at no price. Though parents could sense these characteristics in their children, Adler was the first to elevate the discussion to a clinical investigation, to an analytical study of data based upon observed behavior. He became recognized as the master in dealing with children in these situations and always with an eye towards their constructive education, thus becoming the darling of American educators.*

Both of these types are hardly ever good fellow human beings. The first type (the strong youngest child) fares better in a world where competition is valued for itself. A man of this type will maintain his spiritual equilibrium only at the cost of others, whereas individuals of the second (the weak youngest child) remain under the oppressive feeling of their inferiority and suffer from their lack of reconciliation with life as long as they life.

The oldest child also has well-defined characteristics.

For one thing he has the advantage of an excellent position for the development of his psychic life. History recognizes that the oldest son has had a particularly favorable position. Even where this tradition has not actually become crystallized ... the oldest child is usually the one whom one accredits with enough power and common sense to be the helper or foreman of his parents. If his development in this direction goes on without disturbance then we shall find him with the traits of a guardian of law and order. *Adler was especially sensitive, owing to his own personal life story, to the reality of this dominance of the first son as he was himself the subject of such an older brother. His further remarks regarding the "second-born child" are most insightful and led him to the development of one of his most important contributions to psychotherapeutic practice, namely, the concept of the inferiority complex. He says of the second born son: "The second born may place his goal so high that he suffers from it his whole life, annihilates his inner harmony in following, not the veritable facts of life, but an evanescent fiction and the valueless semblance of things."*

The only child, of course, finds himself in a very particular situation. He is at the utter mercy of the educational methods of his environment. ... Being constantly the center of attention he very easily acquires the feeling that he really counts for something of great value. ... Parents of "only" children are frequently exceptionally cautious people who have themselves experienced life as a great danger, and therefore approach their child with an inordinate solicitude. *Birth order, as we have said, played a major role in Adler's child psychiatry and whether dealing with youngest or oldest child or the only child, he was most sensitive to the personality developmental issues which arise from the birth order phenomenon both as it relates to the individual child's self-understanding as well as that of the child's nurturing environment controlled by parents and teachers.*

We see, therefore, that the very position of the child in the family may lend shape and color to all the instincts, tropisms, faculties and the like, which he brings with him into the world. ... (therefore) it would seem to us that the theory of inheritance of acquired characteristics is based upon very weak evidence. ... From our previous descriptions we may assume that whatever the errors to which a child is exposed in his development, the most serious consequences arise from his desire to elevate himself over all his fellows, to seek more personal power which will give him advantages over his fellow man. *Unlike Freud's rather positive emphasis upon the inevitability of the "will to pleasure" which he felt was the fundamental driving force in human life, Adler is keen both to point out that the "will to power" is, rather, the driving force but, rather than being merely positive about this drive, Adler believes that the social environment, particularly the parents and educators of small children must assert themselves for the controlling and direction of this power-surge for superiority over the child's peers.*

In our culture he is practically compelled to develop according to a fixed pattern. If we wish to prevent such a perilous development we must know the difficulties he has to meet and understand them. There is one single and essential point of view which helps us to overcome all these difficulties; it is the viewpoint of the development of the social feeling. If this development succeeds, obstacles are insignificant, but since the opportunities for this development are relatively rare in our culture, the difficulties which a child encounters play an important role. *Adler is painfully aware of the developmental obstacles placed in the child's path by his social environment, and he rails against parental practices of feeding the drive to dominant, which our culture seems to cherish and perpetuate. In "understanding human nature," Adler is eager for the informed parent and educational system to be aware of the drive or will to power which characterizes human nature and the absolute necessity of guiding and educating that drive for the welfare of human society. The notion of "social feeling," which Adler has so emphasized in his work, is central to this guidance.*

THEORIES AND CONCEPTS

Individual psychology, as we have seen, maintains that the overriding motivation in most individuals is a striving for what Adler early on called superiority but later modified to compensational behavior for feelings of inferiority. This human quest, commencing in early childhood, for self-realization, completeness, and perfection, is usually frustrated by feelings of inadequacy, or incompleteness arising from physical defects, low social status, pampering or neglect during childhood, and not infrequently birth-order. Com-pensational behavior relative to these feelings of inferiority can include the development of personal skills and abilities.

Here is the arena for the parent and the educator to take the initiative in nurturing positive responses to the child's need for a sense of fulfillment even in the face of stifling environmental and physical handicaps. Overcom-pensation for inferiority feelings can, says Adler, take the form of an egocentric striving for power and self-aggrandizing behavior at other's expense. This led Adler to propose an alternative to Freud's short-hand notion of the "will to pleasure" with his own idea of the "will to power." Simplistic and unfair to his own system of thought, this notion nevertheless emphasized the prominence in child development of feelings of inferiority and compensatory behavioral responses to assert jurisdiction over one's own life and destiny, namely, the will to power.

Adler was internationally recognized and acclaimed for his creative and innovative response to the need for the cultivation and monitoring of mental health among children. He has established a series of child-guidance clinics in Vienna in 1921 for this purpose and international figures including Maria Montessori called attention to his outstanding efforts in this regard. Though the Nazi influence on the Austrian government forced the closing of these Adlerian child counseling centers in 1934, his reputation preceded him to New York in 1926, joining first the Columbia University faculty the next year and eventually the faculty of Long Island College of Medicine in 1932.

It is the contention within Individual Psychology that there is a direct relationship between the human person and the world around him as relates particularly to a few biological principles operative within human nature. Psychoneurosis, then, is seen as a disturbance in the re-lationship between the individual and his social environment. Therefore, therapeutics based on individual psychological data must be an etiological therapeutic in the proper sense of that word. Given the social etiology of mental disease, it is the intention of the psychotherapist in the modality of Individual Psychology to address the need for a readjustment of the interpersonal relationship between the patient and his social environment, the community and social circle within which he lives and works and loves.

The term "Individual Psychology" was chosen by Adler specifically to identify his system of theory and analysis because of his radical emphasis upon the essential subjective nature of the individual's striving, the innate creativity of human psychological adaptation, and the wholeness of the individual's unified personality. The drive for superiority in the face of compensatory behavioral response to personal feelings of inferiority constitutes the matrix of human development. "The goal of superiority, with each individual," says Adler, "is personal and unique. It depends upon the meaning he gives to life; and this meaning is not a matter of words. It is built up in his style of life and runs through it like a strange melody of his own creation." If individuals have developed a health social life through creative and responsible interests, their strivings for superiority will be shaped into a style of life that is warmly receptive of others and focused on friendship and interpersonal ties. If not, neuroses and psychoses will develop as the individual attempts to adjust his will to power, his personal agenda, to the conflicting demands and expectations of society.

Individual Psychology is built upon the notion of a

fundamental unity of the human personality. All apparent dichotomies and multiplicities of life are organized in one self-consistent totality. No definite division can be made between mind and body, consciousness and unconsciousness, or between reason and emotion. All behavior is seen in relation to the final goal of superiority or success, of the will to power. This goal gives direction to the individual within his social matrix. If he has developed strong "social feelings" for his social environment, he will thrive. If not, mental illness awaits him as he struggles unsuccessfully to assert his demand for superiority in the absence of a capacity to get along in his social environment due to the failure to have cultivated this strong social feeling.

In contrast to Freud and psychoanalysis, which places so much emphasis upon the assumption that man is motivated by instincts, and in contradistinction to Carl Jung's analytical psychology which emphasizes above all else man's depend-ence upon inborn archetypes, Adler believed that the human person is motivated by social urges. We are inherently social beings and our very nature is interpersonal, requiring cooperation in social activities. Whereas Freud relied upon sexuality and Jung upon primordial thought patterns, Adler stressed social interest or, what we have seen him call, "social feeling."

Furthermore, with respect to the emergence and development of personality, Adler placed emphasis upon the concept of the "creative self," the notion that the human is a highly personalized, subjective entity which interprets his social environment and tries to make sense out of it for his survival and betterment. Whereas Freud would have us believe that personality relies upon inborn instincts for self-aggrandizement, Adler believes that the human person seeks for experienced which will aid in fulfilling the individual's unique style of life. This concept of the "creative self" was new to psychoanalysis but over time has become a major conceptual framework in analyzing personality and behavioral disorders.

A primary distinction of Individual Psychology *vis a vis*

psychoanalysis was Adler's insistence upon the absolute "uniqueness" of each personality. Each person is a composite of his own personalized motivations, traits, interests, and values and each person, then, carries a distinctive style of life unique to his experiences and situation in the social environment. Adler minimalizes Freud's emphasis upon sexual instinct as the dominant dynamic in human behavior, rather calling attention to man's social character, his experiences of inferiorities not sexually derived or driven. Adler's "dethronement" of sexuality was for many professionals and the laity a welcome relief from the monotonous pansexualism of the psychoanalysts in the Freudian camp.

It was upon personal consciousness as the center of human personality which Adler emphasized, studied, and was fascinated by. The human person is a conscious being, ordinarily aware of his reasons for his behavior. Fully cognizant of his inferiorities and well aware of his personal goals for which he strives in life, man is a being capable of planning and guiding his behavior fully conscious of the meaning of such plans as relates to his self-realization as a person. Freud was completely at odds with this concept of personality and image of human nature for Freud and his school felt that human consciousness was a minimal component of human behavior with the individual primarily victimized by his unconsciousness.

Adlerian psychology is quite splendidly simple in terms of the minimal use of conceptual terms developed in his theories of personality. Six major concepts are operative within Individual Psychology and we will quickly review them here. They are (1) fictional finalism, (2) striving for superiority, (3) inferiority feelings and compensation, (4) social interests, (5) style of life, and (6) the creative self.

Once Adler and the Individual Psychology school of professionals distanced themselves from Freud and the psychoanalytic school of psychotherapy, they moved to adopt a rather well developed philosophical optimism, a kind of "idealistic positivism" over against Freud's rather dark notion of "historical determinism." Man, Adler argued, is motivated more by his hopes and aspirations about the future than he is by suppressed experiences of the past. The hopes and aspirations are not teleological, that is, they are not predestined or subject to fate, but rather are quite decidedly subjective, mental constructs of the hope personality. Adler called these "fictional goals," because they are subjective causations which may or may not be realized but are, nevertheless, ever present in the human heart. Rather than teleological in nature and, thus, the result of causation, the fictional nature of hopes and aspirations are based on the principle of finalism. Adler spoke to this issue decisively: *"Individual Psychology insists absolutely on the indispensability of finalism for the understanding of all psychological phenomena. Causes, powers, instincts, impulses, and the like cannot serve as explanatory principles. The final goal alone can explain man's behavior. Experiences, traumata, sexual development mechanisms cannot yield an explanation, but the perspective in which these are regarded, the individual way of seeing them, which subordinates all life to the final goal, can do it."*

Adler was concerned primarily with the fundamental goal in an individual's life, that for which a person strives and results in a kind of consistency of personality, a unity of purpose and person. Even before he left Freud's crowd behind, he had come to the conclusion that "aggression" rather than "sexuality" was the driving force to the human person seeking fulfillment. These aggressive impulses of the human person result in what became known as the "will to power." A child of the time, Adler believed that masculinity was a sign of strength; femininity a sign of weakness. He developed a concept out of this called the "masculine protest" which simply meant that men develop a behavioral mode of response to life's situations called "overcompensation." This is the standard mode of operation when either a man or woman feels helpless or inferior or inadequate. This will to power notion was given up in deference to a more sophisticated concept of the "striving for superiority." From aggression to power to superiority, Individual Psychology evolved into a more refined system of analysis. Not social distinction, leadership, or even a pre-eminent position in society, superiority for Adler in this analytical scheme simply means an endemic drive towards perfection, the "great upward drive" as he called it which characterizes every person, healthy or ill. "I began to see clearly in every psychological phenomenon the striving for superiority" Adler said. "It lies at the root of all solutions of life's problems and is manifested in the way in which we meet these problems." The drive is innate to the human animal.

The etiology of this innate drive, Adler believed, was located in the feelings of inferiority which characterize every person in some form or another and in varying degrees of intensity. Early on in his medical training and beginning clinical work, he links the notion of what he called "organ inferiority" with "overcompensation." He later broadened the concept to include any feelings of inferiority which arose from subjectively felt psychological or social disabilities as well as from physical insufficiencies. Adler believed that feelings of inferiority are the basis for all human improvements and creativity in the world. When these feelings are exaggerated, mental illness is the results. When they are held at bay or educated into a viable selfunderstanding, they lead to success and leadership, superiority of deed and person. Though not inevitably or even commonly leading to pleasure, such development was designed to lead the individual toward perfection which, he believed, was the ultimate goal of life.

The idea of social interest, or social feeling as we discussed earlier in this chapter, came later to Adler and in response to pervasive criticism from the professionals in the field of counseling and therapy. The criticism was due to Adler's early emphasis upon aggression and the will to power at the expense, it was thought, of human cooperation. Because in his own life he was an outspoken proponent of social justice and social democracy, he worked tirelessly to broaden his understanding of human nature to include this sense of social interest and social feeling toward one's fellow man and fellow creatures. Cooperation, he began to say, is a fundamental characteristic of the human person. In this development, he moved further and further away from his earlier emphasis upon aggression and selfish interest, arguing, in his mature years for the centrality of social feeling as an indispensable component of personality.

"Style of life" became a slogan for Adlerians of the day. His whole theory of human personality was summed up in this one expression. Though every person has the goal of superiority (defined in the Adlerian sense of personal pursuit of perfection) as his foremost agenda, there are countless ways in which this superiority might be realized in one's life. The style of life one lives is early formed in childhood. Based upon social encounters with the outside world as well as birth order and family life, the style of life is constructed. His attitudes, feelings, apperceptions, and aspirations are set in motion. One's sense of inferiority in various aspects of life are contributing factors in the development of one's style of life always within the context of self-aware inferiorities and the self-administered pressure to seek perfection and personal fulfillment in one's life. It was the concept of the "creative self" which proved to be the crowning achievement of his theory of personality. All of his other concepts and notions about personality development fell into place when the idea of the creative self was discovered and expanded upon in his clinical work and theoretical writing. It is this creative self which gives a person meaning in life. It is the active principle of humanity. In essence, the doctrine of a creative self asserts that man makes his own personality. This was Adler's major contribution to personality theory and the one which assured the prominence of Individual Psychology.

Adler's humanistic theory of personality was in direct opposition to Freud's conception of human nature. Characteristics such as altruism, humanitarianism, cooper-ation, creativity, uniqueness, and awareness utilized by Adlerian psychology flew in the face of Freud's materialistic, instinctually driven, unconsciously motivated person. Whereas the Freudians were scandalized by the apparent naïve optimism about the human person, Adler's hopefulness toward the future rang clear in the public eye. Adler's system had arrived in America at a time it was most welcome.

Chapter III

Carl Gustav Jung
and Analytical Psychology

BIOGRAPHICAL SKETCH

Carl Gustav Jung's contributions to personality theory were developed over an extended period of time covering more than fifty years and are fully displayed in his twenty-volume set of collected works edited by H. Read and others from 1953-1979, *The Collected Works of C. G. Jung* published by Princeton University Press. The founder of what is called Analytical Psychology, Jung has been praised and maligned by the intellectual and medical community for most of his productive life and certainly since his death. An early associate of Sigmund Freud, Jung would radically depart from psychoanalysis as he matured in his own thought. Without doubt, his original insights lie in a profound awareness of the powerful influence of myths and symbols on the human psyche. The reciprocity of symbol making and using — symbols make man and man makes symbols — constitutes a significant starting point in the study of Jung.

We will here discuss Jung's life, a major text in his massive corpus of writings, and we will review some key concepts in his system of thought called Analytical Psychology. Let us begin with an extended quote to set the stage for our enquiry:

Anyone who wants to know the human psyche will learn next to nothing from experimental psychology. He would be better advised to abandon exact science, put away his scholar's gown,

*bid farewell to his study, and wonder with human heart through
the world. There in the horrors of prisons, lunatic asylums and
hospitals, in drab suburban pubs, in brothels and gambling-halls,
in the salons of the elegant, the Stock Exchanges, socialist
meetings, churches, revivalist gatherings and ecstatic sects,
through love and hate, through the experience of passion in every
form in his own body, he would reap richer stores of knowledge
than textbooks a foot thick could give him, and he will know how
to doctor the sick with a real knowledge of the human soul.* —
Carl Gustav Jung

In a little town located on Lake Constance in the Canton
of Thurgau in Switzerland named Kesswyl, Carl Gustav Jung
was born on July 26, 1875. He was the fourth and only surviving
child of Johann Paul Achilles Jung (1842-1896) and Emilie
Preiswek Jung (1848-1923). Johann was a poor rural clergyman
in the Swiss Reformed Church and Emilie was a member of a
long-established Basel family of distinction and wealth. Taught
Latin by his father and the teachings of exotic religions by his
mother, Carl grew up in an atmosphere of learning and curiosity
with deep sensitivities to mysticism and the occult.

From Carl's birthplace, the family moved when he was
six months to a better parish in Laufen in an effort to better their
living situation. Paul felt the pressure to please his wife of wealth
and breeding and the tensions continued to mount between them.
Emilie was not a well person and whether it was strictly emotional
or had a biogenic origin, it was not certain, though she did spend
some time hospitalized in Basel for several months after the move
to Laufen. At home, she spent a great deal of time in her separate
bedroom from Paul where she believed she was regularly visited
by spirits which visited her at night. Maternal affection was rare
and episodic and eventually Carl was taken by his father to live
with Emilie's unmarried sister in Basel for a time but eventually
returned to his father's home.

Eccentric and depressed, Emilie's bouts of depression

and moodiness had a negative impact upon Jung's perception of womanhood which affected his entire life and work. Jung would later be heard to say that women were essentially "innately unreliable." His father, Paul, was eventually called to another parish in 1879 at Kleinhuningen which, happily, brought Emilie closer to her own family and proved most beneficial in lifting her spirits as the depression gradually dissipated.

Not surprisingly given his birth and early life situation, Jung proved to be a solitary and very introverted child, believing, as he explained in his autobiographical reflections, that he actually had two distinct personalities. The first one, what he called "Personality Number One," was a modern Swiss citizen attuned to the 18th century, and was a typical schoolboy living in that time period. "Personality Number Two" was, however, a dignified authoritarian and an influential person from the past. Much of this early self-indulgence would revisit him in his mature years of theory building. At this time, Jung became painfully aware that he was somewhat disappointed in his father's lack of intellectual acumen in the assessment of the meaning and nature of religion and his approach to a faith-based life.

During his adolescent years, he attended the Humanistisches gymnasium in Basel. During his first year as a student there, age twelve, he was roughed up by another boy and a severe fall to the ground caused a momentary unconsciousness. This experience led him to believe that he would not now ever have to attend school again and when he was being told it was time to leave for school, he regularly fainted. Staying home, then, for six months, Jung at first enjoyed the power and the freedom of his situation. However, when he overheard his father explaining to a colleague that he feared Carl would never be able to support himself because of possible epilepsy, Carl was shocked back into facing reality and the inevitable need for academic achievement if true financial freedom was to ever be his. He rallied, commenced vigorously studying his father's Latin grammar text and, though he fainted three times in the process, he eventually overcame the urge and proved a distinguished student after all.

In his adult reflections, Jung sites this as the occasion when "I learned what a neurosis is." His studies, particularly of Krafft-Ebing's book entitled *Psychopathia Sexualis*, persuaded him to specialize in psychiatric medicine when he pursued his university education. He studied medicine at the Universities of Basel and Zurich with strong emphasis in biology, zoology, paleontology, and archaeology, all the while as a medical student working with patients in the training hospital. Studying psychiatric patients closely and employing what he would call word associations to which patients responded in what he called "complexes," he began his long journey towards his fundamental theories of Analytical Psychology. Interestingly enough, he combined a passion for psychiatry with an equal passion for the humanities, myths, symbols, and esotericisms of all kinds (somewhat reflective of his own mother's preoccupations). As a young intern, he became a staff physician at Zurich's Burgolzli Psychiatric Hospital where he applied his method of free association which proved clinically helpful in his identifying of repressed complexes among the mentally ill in his care. He became acquainted with Freud's work upon reading *The Interpretation of Dreams*, while studying under the psychiatrist Eugen Bleuler who as a strong proponent of the new "psycho-analysis" just emerging out of Vienna.

In 1903 when he was finishing up his medical school training and looking to establish himself as a psychiatrist in Basel, he married Emma Rauschenbach, a young lady from one of the wealthiest family in all of Switzerland. Five children were born to Carl and Emma: Agathe, Gret, Franz, Marianne, and Helene. Though the married lasted fifty-two years, until Emma's death in 1955, it was not always calm and serene as Jung was very want to have many relationships outside of married with women who came and went in his life and practice. Two of the most renowned extramarital partners Jung had, going so far as having them in his own on a regular basis, were Sabina Spielrein and

Toni Wolff. These relationships were fully known by Emma and, owing to Jung's persuasive powers, agreed or at least tolerated them, Emma herself becoming a therapist in the process. Following Jung's publishing of his controversial book, *Answer to Job*, Jung established a life-long friendship with a Catholic priest from England named Father Victor White.

When Jung was thirty-one years old and in full service as a psychiatrist doing clinical work and research at the hospital, he published *Studies in Word Association* based upon his own analysis of mentally ill patients and the use of his developing method of word association as a key tool in the treatment plan. He sent a copy of this work to Sigmund Freud which resulted in the beginning of an acquaintance, not really a friendship, which would have historic ramifications for psychoanalysis and psychotherapeutic history. Their relationship lasted six years during which time Freud became convinced that Jung was the heir apparent to lead psychoanalysis into the new century.

However, six years later in 1912, Jung published the book that would essentially bring their mutual respect and working relationship to a halt. Jung published *Wandlungen und Symbole der Libido (*English translation in 1916, *The Psychology of the Unconscious).* They both contended their system of analysis was right and the other wrong and, like Freud had done earlier in his career, Jung went through a very severe psychological storm similar to Freud's which he called "neurasthenia and hysteria." For Jung, the break with Freud was further exacerbated with the coming first World War and the troubles in Europe which affected all medical, and especially psychiatric, practice in Austria, Switzerland, and Germany.

Within three years of making Freud's acquaintance, Jung was made editor of the newly founded publication of Freud's professional group called the *Yearbook for Psycho-analytical and Psychopathological Research.* Two years later Jung was also appointed by Freud and his colleagues Chairman for Life of the *International Psychoanalytical Association.* Troubles began to emerge as Freud and Jung began to challenge each others views on religion and the libido.

Jung had become increasingly dissatisfied with Freud's heavy, even inordinate, emphasis upon sexual interpretations of the libido which, Freud argued, showed origins from infancy. Jung rather emphasized the close parallels between ancient myths and psychotic fantasies and by explaining human motivation in terms of a larger creative energy. Stepping down from the presidency of the International Psychoanalytic Society, Jung, like Adler before him, established his own professional body for Analytical Psychology. Jung moved his clinical practice to his home in the village of Kenssett on the shores of Lake Zurich where patients from all over the world, attracted to him by his increasingly voluminous publications. Abandoning Freud's famous "couch therapy," Jung chose to have his patients sit in a chair facing him for interactive dialogue. "I confront the patient as one human being to another," Jung explained, because "analysis is a dialogue demanding two partners; the doctor has something to say but so has the patient."

When Clark University invited Sigmund Freud to come to America to receive an honorary doctorate in 1909, Carl Jung was likewise invited to attend, though not to be so honored. Jung was only thirty years old when he published the book that gained him Freud's attention, namely, *Studies in Word Association.* But at their first meeting, they talked thirteen hours straight according to Freud's wife and children. Freud was then fifty years old and this relationship, based on similar interests and a mutual desire to create something new, last six years, ending in May of 1910, the year after the visit to America. Their last face-to-face meeting was in 1913 in Munich where Jung gave a lecture on psychological types, the introverted and extraverted type, in Analytical Psychology. This constituted the introduction of some of the key concepts which came to distinguish Jung's work from Freud's for the next half century. The break was final but not clean. Jung suffered considerably over the next many years and his isolation from professional life outside his little world of patients and writing exacerbated his mental health considerably.

Their primary disagreement, at the end of the day and after all issues related to competing strong egos have subsided, has to do with the theory of the unconscious. Jung differed from Freud whose theory of the unconscious appeared to Jung to be incomplete and unnecessarily negative. Freud conceived the unconscious solely as a repository of repressed emotions and desires, or at least that is the way Jung saw Freud's thought. Agreeing with Freud about the personal unconscious, Jung also believed in a collective unconscious where the archetypes of primordial experience reside. Freud would have none of it.

Unlike Freud, who preferred to stay and work strictly at home and, we should remember, suffered severely from cancer, Jung, on the other hand, became extremely active following World War I, not publishing massive tomes of clinical and speculative studies but traveling extensively, thanks to the wealth his wife inherited as well as his medical fees from rich patients and his publications.

Patients and the public were fascinated with his passion for analyzing the unconscious, not so much for the "dirt" which Freud would believe to be the cause of mental illness, but for the mystery, awe, and excitement of delving into one's own inner self to discover who a person really is to himself. This was popularization of depth psychology at its most marketable best! After thirty books and hundreds of articles on the unconscious, Jung was the acclaimed master of the field. He believed in the power of dreams to interpret the workings of the unconscious. Dreams symbolize ignored or rejected aspects of our own personality, and we want to know what these are. "The dream," Jung wrote, "is the small hidden door in the deepest and most intimate sanctum of the world, which opens to that primeval cosmic night that was soul long before there was conscious ego and will be soul far beyond what a conscious ego could ever reach."

Jung's world travels allowed him to study a wide variety of religions, myths, and symbol systems. Likewise drawing from his patients' recounted dreams and their recurring symbols, Jung developed the concept of the "collective unconsciousness," later refining the concept to distinguish between the personal unconscious, or the repressed feelings and thought developed during an individual's life, and the collective unconscious, or those inherited feelings, thoughts, and memories shared by all humanity. "The unconscious is not just evil by nature, it is also the source of the highest good," Jung wrote, "not only dark but also light, not only bestial, semi human, and demonic but superhuman, spiritual, and, in the classical sense of the word, 'divine'." This "collective" is comprised, said Jung, of the "archetypes" of humanity, the primordial images, occurring time and time again in symbols of religion, myths, fairy tales, and fantasies.

Lecturing while visiting North Africa and the United States, among other places, he delivered famous Terry Lectures at Yale University in 1938 which were published as *Psychology and Religion*. His visit to India, among all else, led him to become fascinated and deeply involved with Hindu philosophy, and the process developing key concepts in his analytical psychology which integrated spirituality with studies of the unconscious. Jung believed, based upon his clinical studies and self-analysis, that life has a spiritual purpose beyond material goals. The human person's primary responsibility, then, is to discover and fulfill these innate potentials which must be identified and owned through the process of dream analysis. Furthermore, he believed that this spiritual journey of self-transformation is at the heart of the great world religions, particularly as articulated in their respective mystical traditions. This "inward journey" was designed for the individual to meet the self while simultaneously and thereby meeting the Divine. Unlike Freud, Jung felt that spiritual experience was indispensable to the well-being of the person and the dream provided access to this inward journey

There are two kinds of dreams, according to Jung. There is the "Big" dream where the poetic force and beauty that occurs mostly during the critical stages of life such as puberty, onset of middle age and within sight of death. The "Little" dreams were those dealing with everyday occur-rences. Jung placed great, even grave, importance upon dream content, particularly as he was able to connect the dream's symbols with the archetypal symbols of our primordial unconscious. The dream can be a major source of enlightenment and guidance to the listing, caring individual.

Jung was eighty-seven years old when he died on June 6, 1961, in his little village of Kensett. With thirty books and hundreds of articles published, he was world renowned and world acclaimed. He had traveled the world but towards the end wanted only to stay in a little stone tower he had built near his home in Switzerland. Widowed and with all his children gone away, he continued to see a few patients and continued to write. Though Freud had lived to rejoice at the death of Alfred Adler, Jung outlived Freud by six years and did not, like Freud, rejoice at the passing of his old friend and adversary.

THE CLASSIC TEXT CONSIDERED

Jung got busy and stayed busy, from the time he commenced his medical school training until his final demise, Jung was forever researching and writing, developing clinical modalities of treatment and producing conceptual frame-works for his analysis. It took thirty books and hundreds of articles for Jung to say it all. And, to be frank, he never suggested that he did say it all. Any one text of his published library could arguably be called a classic in its own right, but we have chosen his 1921 book, *Psychological Types*, for our attention here. At the time of its writing, Jung says he was working diligently upon the question, "what does one do with the unconscious?" His answer, he reported, was related to function of the ego and its role in balancing the personal unconscious and the collective unconscious.

He says in his autobiography that he was simultaneously busy with preparatory work for *Psychological Types*, first published in 1921. "This work," he wrote, sprang originally from my need to define the ways in which my outlook differed from Freud's and Adler's." He came across the problem of "types" in addressing this fundamental distinction between Analytical Psychology and that of both Psychoanalysis and Personal Psychology. "It is one's psychological type," he suggests, which from the outset determines and limit's a person's judgment. My book," he continues, "was an effort to deal with the relationship of the individual to the world, to people and things." This work yielded the insight that, says Jung, "every judgment made by an individual is conditioned by his personality type and that every point of view is necessarily relative."

Some have argued that these early musings about types derived from his Burgholzli experiences in dealing with differing patterns of hysterical and schizophrenic patients. Where as hysterics find meaning in the outside world of objects (what Jung called a "centrifugal movement of libido"), schizophrenics, on the other hand, seek meaning within the inner world of their own making through dreams, fanatises, and archetypes (suggesting to Freud a "centripetal tendency of libido"). The former Jung came to label as a type called "extravert" and the later a type called "introvert." H. Crichton-Miller of the Institute of Medical Psychology in London chose rather, in his 1933 book *psychoanalysis and its Derivatives* to trace Jung's interest in types to a 1896 book by Francis Jordan entitled, *Character as Seen in Body and Parentage.* Jung read this book in 1914 when it was brought to his attention by one of his first English disciplines, Dr. Constance Long. Jung was at this time wrestling with the problem of inherited psychic traits and was baffled as to how to organize his thoughts on the subject.

Probably from both Burgholzli and Jordan, Jung began toying with the concept of psychological "type" and eventually evolved his now world famous schema of types and sub-types. The bipolar nature of extravert and introvert worked splendidly in his overall schematic. The extravert is primarily directed outwards; the introvert inwards. The extravert is self-expressive whereas the introvert has difficulty in articulation. The extravert is self-seeking in his liking of other people including being a propagandist if necessary; the introvert is detached and self-content to go it alone. The extravert prefers publicity and social interaction; the introvert prefers solitude. From all of this we gather that the extravert is gregarious whereas the introvert is a solitary figure.

From these two main types which are called "general attitude-types," Jung proceeds to a further subdivision of four primary functions, namely, thinking, feeling, intuition and sensation. Every person, Jung argued, possesses these four functions of the psyche, though everyone has a "dominant side" and a "subordinate side," or superior and inferior, when it comes to the functioning of introversion and extraversion. By pairing introversion with the four primary functions of thinking, feeling, intuition, and sensation, and pairing extraversion with thinking, feeling, intuition, and sensation, Jung came up with eight essential personality types. In order to fully appreciate the dynamic insight Jung brought to personality theory, we will spend a moment to characterize each of these eight personality types. Based upon the fundamental principles developed by Jung's concept of personality types, the Myers-Briggs and other personality tests have had a field day during the past fifty or so years. Let us consider each of the eight types briefly here by way of summary.

The *introverted thinker*, given the rationalistic externality of his subjective bias towards facts, Jung believed, is actually more taken with the idea of factual reality than with the facts themselves. Essentially theoretical, he is gifted with an attitude of aloofness and distance bordering on arrogance. Feelings being held at bay, intuition languishes and he struggles with maintaining any sustained friendships but rather embraces a defensive attitude akin to dogmatism and intellectual self-assertion. Commitment to the moral code is strong and a high level of rigidity and intolerance color his attitudes towards the rules of the game.

The *extraverted thinker* is, likewise, a rationalist and is intolerant and fanatical in his relentless pursuit of facts, the truth, the correct way of things. Discounting opposition, he is always in quest of a formula and promotes it when he finds it or creates it. Found prominently among professional politicians, his convictions are tied to his personal belief that he is right, he has found the answer, his way of logical analysis solves all problems. "Ought" and "must" are paramount in their assessment of their duty. Not fearing criticism, he leans towards the sciences and the exactitude of objective analysis of data. Often numbered among the scientists, he method is to gather the facts as he understands and perceives them and then to produce a theory based upon his findings.

The *feeling introvert* is more often, says Jung, found among rationalistic women who appear to others as cold and distant from their feelings and the feelings of others. Appearing to disregard the feelings and opinions of others, there is a hint of superiority and critical neutrality in their social relations. Living by "affective valuation," their likes and dislikes are clearly identified and stated, they love and hate with equal passion and intensity but are deficient in expressing these feelings. More than other types of introverts, they fear and loath the thought of being dominated by outside forces. Though considered by others as cold and hard, they in reality are neither but fail to show their true selves for fear of domination by the outside world.

The *feeling extravert* is, says Jung, also more prevalent among women. These individuals are objective, conventional, and social. They enjoy and admire the common things of society. As an extreme counter to introverted personalities, they are extremely expressive of their feelings. Extremely suggestible by the social environment, their responses are often exaggerated in their attempt to reach a conformity to their social world. They make friends easily and are thereby greatly influenced by their friends' attitudes and values. Intense, effervescent, and sociable, these are the dominant characteristics of the feeling extravert.

The *sensorial introvert* "appreciates the good things of life" but is essentially irrational and is, therefore, often dominated by the changing flux of external events. Dominated by their susceptibility to objective reality, their personal feelings and responses are uppermost in their guiding responses to life. They assess the world, its demands, its ethical dilemmas, its surprises, with sensorial emotion, always personalizing the objective into something related and relevant only to themselves personally.

The *sensorial extravert* actively seeks out new and provocative experiences in the world for his life is entirely conditioned by his objective environment. He is the most easily bored of Jung's psychological types for his personal resources are minimal and undervalued by himself. Constant external stimulus is his delight and demand, and he has no patience with any pursuit or theory that involves the abstract. A discriminating critic of sense impressions, they become connoisseurs of wine, art, poetry, and all things perceived as refined by the wider culture. Considered by all to be good company, they are realistic, sensual, jolly, and a social delight though devoid of personal intuition and objectivity.

The *intuitive introvert* is the exact opposite of the sensorial extravert and is singularly devoid of external facts. The world of the intuitive introvert is decidedly subjective and devoid of any concern for what others might call objective reality. Appearing to be aloof and unconcerned about the outside world of deeds and facts, they come across as slightly mad or debilitating artistic to their own detriment. Concentrating upon the creation of their own interior world, they often come across as a crank or oddball. Mystic, dreamer, and eccentric are characteristic terms for the intuitive introvert.

The *intuitive extravert* is pronouncedly unstable, always seeking change and something different. Constancy is taboo and his quest for the new, the different, the ever-changing world around him leaves the impression that he is an optimist. Flighty is a common term for such individuals as they jump from one idea to another, one activity to another, never really finishing anything but ever questing for something new and different. Often and to no one's surprise, their decisions often are good ones even if they are unable to stay the course. They inspire people with their vision, their capacity to imagine a new and better world. Visionary, changeable, and creative are characteristic terms for the intuitive extravert.

His book on the subject, *Psychological Types,* catapulted him into world fame and the practical results of these ideas produced a plethora of personality tests, some based upon Jung's own eight types while other psychometrists produced their own types and categories. The idea, however, of being able to divide and subdivide the human personality into identifiable and testable characteristics caught on and is still very much with us.

THEORIES AND CONCEPTS

The path to self-knowledge, the goal of all therapy, Jung believed, lies in expanding the perimeters of human consciousness. We are too narrow, too restricted, to self-protective in our thinking about life and our investigation of our inner selves. This quest for self-knowledge, Jung believed, was essentially the nature of human culture. "Attainment of consciousness is culture in the broadest sense, and self-knowledge is therefore the very essence of this process." The emphasis in Jung's work, writings, and therapy was all upon the need for "a personal, contemporary consciousness, but also a supra-personal consciousness with a sense of historical continuity." the psyche according to Jung "is a self-regulating system that maintains its equilibrium just as the body does. Every process," he explains, "that goes too far immediately and inevitably calls forth compensations, and without these there would be neither a normal metabolism nor a normal psyche." It is the psychic balance of conscious and unconscious materials which the ego seeks to monitor and nurture in the mentally healthy person.

Before we explore Jung's concept of consciousness, we are required to investigate the composites of the "psyche," which, says Jung, consists of three components, viz., the ego, the personal unconscious which includes its complexes, and the collective unconscious which includes its archetypes, the persona, the anima or animus, and the shadow. "A more or less superficial layer of the unconscious," wrote Jung in 1934, "is undoubtedly persona. I call it the 'personal unconscious.' But this personal layer rests upon a deeper layer, which does not derive from personal experience and is not a personal acquisition but is inborn. This deeper layer I call the 'collective unconscious'. I have chosen the term 'collective' because this part of the unconscious is not individual but universal; in contrast to the personal psyche, it has contents and modes of behavior that are more or less the same everywhere and in all individuals."

These three conceptual components of the human mind, viz., the ego, the personal unconscious, and the collective unconscious, also embodies the characteristics of introversion and extraversion, the functions of thinking, feeling, sensing, and intuiting, and, finally, the self which is the fully developed and fully unified personality in search of self-actualization.

The ego, for Jung, is the conscious mind and is the center of personality and personality, says Jung, is essentially of two types driving the individual in either the direction of "extraversion" or "introversion" leading Jung to suggest that all people can be divided into these two groups. The ego, he argues, consists of conscious thinking, feeling, sensing, and intuiting. To these four psychological functions of personality must be added, then, the two orientations of extraversion and introversion, making it possible for eight personality types: thinking introvert, thinking extravert, feeling introvert, feeling extravert, and so on.

The ego, unlike Freud's mere executive arbitrator between the id and the superego, is responsible for the individual's feelings of identity and continuity, and is essentially at the center of personality. The personal unconscious is a component of the human mind adjacent but not contiguous with the ego. Its content is comprised of past experiences now forgotten, or ignored, and which failed to make a lasting impression to the conscious mind. This data is all accessible to human consciousness by using the right means of retrieval and there is a great deal of mutual interaction between the personal unconscious and the ego. A grouping of this data in the personal unconscious Jung calls a "complex." A complex is a constellation of feelings, thoughts, perceptions, and memories grouped and sorted in the personal unconscious and may, with proper guidance and effort, be retrieved for analysis, utility, and therapeutic benefit to the individual. The "mother complex" is an example of this grouped constellation of experiences spanning an individual's infancy, childhood, adolescence, and adulthood, all of which are accessible to the ego but deposited in the personal unconscious.

The concept of a collective unconscious, a sort of transpersonal unconscious, is unique to Jung's Analytical Psychology, at least in the fashion in which he has chosen to define and use it. Both original and highly controversial, this concept in Jungian psychology, particularly his personality theory, and it has caused a great deal of stir among clinical psychotherapist and theorists. It is the core and power source of the human psyche and when mental illness appears it dominates both the ego and the personal unconscious. Jung believed the collective unconscious to be the repository of latent memory traces inherited from man's ancestral past, a past that included racial history as an animal species. He called it the storehouse of "psychic residue" of man's evolutionary development and it is almost completely detached from anything personal in the life of an individual, and it is present in all human beings at all times and in all places. It is the foundation, Jung argued, of the whole structure of human personality. Jung says that "the unconscious holds possibilities which are locked away from the conscious mind, for it has at its disposal all subliminal contents, all those things which have been forgotten or overlooked, as well as the wisdom and experience of uncounted centuries, which are laid down in its archetypal organs."

The fundamental foundation of Jung's whole argument for a collective unconscious (that concept which got him into trouble and kept him in trouble throughout his professional life) was, as we have been saying, the notion of "archetype." The human mind sorts our experiences in the ego into clusters based upon the grand categories of primordial archetypes. There are many of these and their origins are from the ancient past of human evolution carried forward from generation to generation, by means of the collective unconscious. For the collective unconscious, Freud used what he called "phylogenic endowment" and placed little importance on its therapeutic value. For Jung, the collective unconscious constituted the core of his analysis and treatment. In his 1934 book, *The Archetypes and the Collective Unconscious,* Jung attempted to address to skeptics and critics of his notion of the archetype particularly as relates to empirical proof of their reality. "We must now turn to the question of how the existence of archetypes can be proved.

Since archetypes are supposed to produce certain psychic forms, we must discuss how and where one can get hold of the material demonstrating these forms. The main source, then, is dreams, which have the advantage of being involuntary, spontaneous products of nature not falsified by any conscious purpose. By questioning the individual one can ascertain which of the motifs appearing in the dream are known to him. ... consequently, we must look for motifs which could not possibly be known to the dreamer and yet behavior functionally of the archetype known from historical sources." Jung, then, in his clinical practice became the great interpreter based upon his incomparable knowledge of the mythic literature and religious symbols of the world.

The ARCHETYPE functions, for Jung, as a center of energy which moved from generation to generation, carried by repetition and continual elaboration in the complex of human experiences. The nucleus of a complex is usually an archetype and the archetype can enter into the personal consciousness of an individual by away of certain types of associated experiences, revealed in the dream or word associations. There are countless archetypes accumulated over the centuries of human development and some of these have such identifiable characteristics as to constitute entities identifiable through analysis, such as in particular the persona, the anima and animus, and the shadow.

The PERSONA is a mask which is put on by an individual in response to demands required of the social environment and tradition and in consort with his own archetypal needs. It constitutes the role society expects him to play and which is, in turn, is willing to play, within reason. When conflict arises, mental illness appears. To the extent that the individual is living in consort with his archetypal inner needs reflected in the persona he has been given and has chosen to adopt, he will remain healthy. The "nucleus" from which the persona develops, then, is one's own archetype.

The ANIMA and the ANIMUS are generally recognized in all branches of the psychological sciences as indicative of the bisexual nature of the human animal. Physiologically, the human animals secretes both male and female sex hormones, and on the psychological level, masculine and feminine characteristics are found in both sexes as well. Man, says Jung, apprehends the nature of woman by virtue of his anima, and woman apprehends the nature of man by virtue of his animus. Mental illness results when there is an imbalance or a disconnect between an individual's "idealized" (archetypal) image of the opposite sex and the reality of that person.

The SHADOW is possibly the most ancient of archetypes and originates from the lowest forms of evolutionary life which we have inherited and, therefore, the Shadow typifies the animal nature of man more than any other and expresses itself in images and ideas of evil, the devil, wickedness and the enemy. It constitutes the content base of feelings of evil thoughts, feelings, and desires within the human person. It is the dark side of a controlled ego and personality must have the energy which derives from the Shadow just as it must home the energy derived from the images of other archetypes such as mother and wise old man.

The SELF is the center of personality and all other components of the human mind form a circling constellation around it. It holds the mental structure in place, providing unity, equilibrium, and stability to the individual's state of mind. The self functions as an archetype and constitute the goal of every person striving for a sense of wholeness and completeness in their lives. Jung believed that true religious experiences are as close as most people get to a fully realized sense of self. Before the fully actualized self can emerge, says Jung, it is necessary for the various components of the personality which we have discussed to become fully developed and individuated. Jung believed that this realization is not possible until at least middle age and more probably old age is the most likely time for the true self to emerge.

SELF-ACTUALIZATION is, says Jung, the fundamental goal of personality development. This occurs only when the person has developed the capacity to differentiate the various systems operative within his psyche, called "individuation," and has realized a harmony of all component parts, called the "transcendent function." When the self has attained to its rightful place as the center of the personality, the self-actualization is realized. It is more a process than a point at which to arrive. This process takes years of intentional effort and usually can occur, if ever, during old age when ego-affirmation behavior has taken a back seat to the quest for self and personal individuation leading to self-actualization of the individual. Jung's therapeutic treatment aimed at reconciling the diversity of personality components, of integrating the points of opposition between extroversion and introversion, between feeling and thinking, sensing and intuiting. The achievement of this integrality of the self leads to an intentioned state of individuality which gives rise to wholeness of self or what Jung called "self-actualization.

Not known for his humility, Jung nevertheless in 1933 wrote in his book, *Modern Man in Search of a Soul,* this: "It is in applied psychology, if anywhere, that today we should be modest and grant validity to a number of apparently contradictory opinions; for we are still far from having anything like a thorough knowledge of the human psyche, that most challenging field of scientific enquiry. For the present, we have merely more or less plausible opinions that defy reconciliation."

Of course, with modern molecular biology and neurobiology, there has been no evidence of such an archetypal primordial residue found in human DNA and, thus, much of Jung's system is called into scientific question though its therapeutic value is still strongly defended by many psychotherapists.

Chapter IV

Viktor Frankl
and Logotherapy

BIOGRAPHICAL SUMMARY

The Third School of Viennese Psychotherapy was established by Viktor Emil Frankl. As with Freud, the founder of the school of Psychoanalysis and with Adler, the founder of the school of Individual Psychology, Frankl was a Jew, a physician, a Neurologist and a native of Vienna. These points of continuity with Freud and Adler are not inconsequential and will appear again and again in the discussion of his life's work more so than in the life work of Freud or Adler. The reason for this are complex and numerous and we will point them out as we explore the world in which logo therapy appeared.

His father and previous ancestors were civil servants (Beamtenfamilie), were moderately practicing Jews and were citizens of Vienna through the good times and bad. Viktor was the middle of three children and, reportedly, knew he wanted to be a physician by the time he was four years old. Frankl became interested in psychology early in his life and at the time of his graduating from the Gymnasium, his leaving paper dealt with the psychology of philosophical thinking. In 1923, he entered the University of Vienna's school of medicine, later choosing to specialize in neurology and psychiatry with depression and suicide his primary fields of concentration. During these years he had personal contact with both Freud and Adler. He went so far as to published an article in Adler's journal on a topic of mutual interest to Frankl and to psychoanalysis.

He was dedicated to his studies and respected by his peers and professional colleagues alike. In 1924, while still a student, he was elected President of the *Skozialistische Mittelschuler Osterreich* which provided the arena in which he and his assistants counseled students during their examination trials, a difficult time for many students when not infrequently students took their life due to failure. On his watch, there was not a single instance of student suicide and this would set the stage for his life's work following his own severe trials in the concentration camps of Hitler's Third Reich.

The immediate result of this great success was his being appointed, following medical school, to head the *Selbstmorderpavillon* (the so-called "suicide pavilion") at the General Hospital in Vienna. During his tenure from 1933-1937 and under his clinical supervision, he and his colleagues treated over 30,000 women prone to suicide. However and commencing in 1938 with the rise of anti-Semitism in Austria, he was prohibited from treating the so-called Aryan patients because he was a Jew. Feeling compelled to move into private practice during these troubled times, he did so but in 1940 he was called to head the neurological department of the Rothschild Hospital where, among other things, he practice as a neurosurgeon in keeping with his medical training. Jews were allowed, indeed, welcomed to practice medicine in this Vienna hospital and it is reported that on countless occasion his medical opinion was crucial in the saving of patients' lives who were otherwise earmarked for euthanasia under the Nazi euthanasia program.

In 1941, he married Tilly Grosser and the very next year, on the 25th of September, he and Tilly, with his parents, were deported to the concentration camp of Theresienstadt where his father died the next year of enforced starvation. While being forced to do day labor, Frankl, along with two distinguished colleagues Dr. Leo Baeck and Regina Jonas, continued to practice medicine as best they could, concentrating primarily upon psychiatric practice as related to depression and suicide. Psychiatry happily did not require much medical paraphernalia and their practice thrived in this inhuman situations.

At Theresienstadt, he was initially assigned to serve as a general practitioner in the clinic for inmates but his psychiatric skills being observed and his training coming to light, he was asked by the camp directors to establish a special unit to help newcomers to the camp overcome shock and grief. From this, he eventually created a suicide watch unit. It is said that during these dark days, he was known to have regularly, upon finishing his day's labor in the suicide unit, stood outside in the cold, lonely darkness giving lectures on various aspects of psychiatric health as a means of maintaining his own sanity and, as he reflected later in life, attempting against all odds to objectify his experience for purposes of scientific analysis and pragmatic assessment of its relevance to the meaning of life.

Frankl was fortunate enough to have been assigned to the psychiatric care ward and was made head of the neurological clinic in Block B IV which had been established and was being maintained as a camp service for psychic hygiene and the mental care of the sick and weary who were suffering primarily from acute depression. Camp rules precluded under pain of punishment any attempt to intervene in a suicide of an inmate at the camp. Interestingly enough and not without its own irony, Frankl was granted permission to host a series of lectures at Theresienstadt on such topics as "Sleep and Its Disturbances," "Body and Soul," "Medical Care of Soul," "Psychology of Mountaineering," "Rax and Schneeberg," "How I Keep My Nerves Healthy," "Existential Problems in Psychotherapy," and "Social Psychotherapy." None of his lectures survived the camp!

During the summer of 1943, Frankl organized a closed-session meeting of the Scientific Society in which he lectured on the topic, "Life-Exhaustion and Life-courage in Terezin." Such a meeting of the camp physicians and scientists being held was extremely dangerous but the hunger for professional conversation overrode any impeding fears they harbored while living and surviving in the death camps. These enduring interests of his in psychotherapy, depression, and life-based issues telegraph his great contribution to mental health research which would eventuate in the development of his system of psychotherapy, first called "existential analysis," and eventually "logotherapy."

In October of 1944, Frankl was transported to Auschwitz. Shortly thereafter, his mother and his brother died in Turkheim, a concentration camp not far from Dachau where Frankl was subsequently transported that same month. Simultaneously, Frankl's wife had been shipped to the Bergen-Belsen concentration camp where she soon died of labor exhaustion and forced starvation as well. Amidst the suffering, humiliation, and deminishment of the value of human life on all fronts, Frankl managed to write a book in manuscript form, namely, *The Doctor and the Soul,* reflecting upon his experiences as a Jew and a psychiatrist in these unbelievable circumstances. The manuscript, alas, was taken from him by the guards even though he attempted to hide it in his clothing. Subsequently, he commenced the rewrite of the document on bits of paper and scraps he stole, sequestering it in the lining of his coat. After the Liberation, it was eventually published and became an internationally acclaimed best seller, namely, *The Doctor and the Soul.*

In the spring of 1945 with the invasion of the Allied Forces into Germany, Frankl was liberated. Of all of his many relatives from Vienna and the rural countryside of Austria, only his sister survived the camps. All others perished before the liberation. Through it all, Frankl continued to believe that even in the midst of the most absurd, painful and dehumanizing situations, life has potential meaning and that even in the midst of such suffering, meaning can be found with proper guidance. This believe was the basis upon which he launched his psychotherapeutic methodology called logotherapy. In his now famous, *Man's Search for Meaning,* Frankl wrote: "If a prisoner felt that he could no longer endure the realities of camp life, he found a way out in his mental life — an invaluable opportunity to dwell in the spiritual domain, the one that the SS were unable to destroy. Spiritual life strengthened the prisoner, helped him adapt, and thereby improved his chances of survival."

Following his three awful years of concentration camp life, Frankl chose to return to Vienna in 1945 during which time he wrote the now famous book, in English titled *Man's Search for Meaning,* but in its original German title was "trotzdem ja zum Leben sagen": *Ein Psychologe erlebt das Konzentrationslager* (translated literally, "...saying yes to life regardless: a Psychologist Experiences the Concentration Camp). Astoundingly and amazingly, this book is a recounting of his concentration experiences from the per-spective of a psychiatrist, an objective observer as medical professional and neurologist. It captured the imagination of all who read it, whether layman or professional.

The next year, 1946, he was appointed director of the Vienna Poliklinik of Neurology and he remained in that position until 1971. The year following his appointment there, he married his second wife, Eleonore Katharina Schwindt, whom, says he, he fell in love with the "first time I saw her" even though he was twice her age. They had one child, a son named Gabriel and a daughter named Gabriele. Nine years following his appointment to the Poliklinik, he was made professor of neurology and psychiatry at the University of Vienna, where he had taken his medical training as a youngster, and was also made a visiting professor while he resided at Harvard University. He won, among many other honors, the Oskar Pfister Prize from the American Society of Psychiatry. He continued to teach until the age of eighty-five and in 1995 completed his autobiography and his final book was published in 1997. Of his thirty-two published books, many have appeared in numerous translations. He is acclaimed, most conspicuously, as the founder (and creator) of logotherapy and he lectured and taught all over the world, receiving twenty-nine honorary doctorates in recognition of his great contribution to psychotherapy and the philosophy of the meaning of life. Frankl died quietly on September 2, 1997, in Vienna, at the age of ninety-two.

From Freud's "will to pleasure" to Adler's "will to power," Frankl believed that logo therapy lead people to an understanding of the "will to meaning," and to this understanding he gave his life's work. Frankl said, "We need to stop asking about the meaning of life, and instead, to think of ourselves as those who were being questioned by life ... Our answer must consist, not in talk and meditation, but in right action and in right conduct. Life ultimately means taking the responsibility to find the right answer to its problems and to fulfill the tasks which it constantly sets for each individual ...It does not really matter what we expect from life; rather, what matters is what life expects from us."

THE CLASSICAL TEXT CONSIDERED

No psychotherapist considered in this study will have published only one book. Some have published many and each has published a few which have gained their international acclaim. Certainly this is true of Viktor Frankl, for his two major books, namely, *The Doctor and the Soul: From Psychotherapy to logotherapy,* and *Man's Search for Meaning*, have established Viktor Frankl as an indisputed authority on psychotherapy in the modern world. So, in all fairness, we will look at both these works as relates to Frankl's Third School of Viennese Psychotherapy. And each, in turn, will be quoted indiscriminately for each of presentation.

In introducing his work, Frankl reports the following: "I remember my dilemma in a concentration camp when faced with a man and a woman who were close to suicide; both had told me that they expected nothing more from life. I asked both my fellow prisoners whether the question was really what we expected from life. Was it not, rather, what life was expecting from us?" The humility of Frankl was often extremely disarming. For example, he once said that "the aim of logo therapy is not to take the place of existing psychotherapy, but only to complement it, thus forming a picture of man in his wholeness — which includes the spiritual dimension." "Spiritual distress" was a concern of his, not religious particularly, but concerned about the inner person. In this sense, he says, "the sense of despair over the meaning of life may be called an *existential neurosis* as opposed to clinical neurosis." Furthermore, he explains, it is conceivable that frustration of the will-to-meaning may also lead to neurosis, what I have chosen to call *existential frustration.*" And, explains Frankl, because 20% of neuroses are noogenic in nature and origin, logo therapy is a specific therapeutic treatment.

Frankl believed that "life has a meaning to the last breath" and even in the midst of the inhumanity of his concentration experience, where, says he, consuming one's own mucus from a cold meant salvaging a few extra calories or peeing on oneself to experience momentarily the pleasure of warmth against one's body or the warmth which came by developing a fever in the work camps, all spoke of our quest for meaning in our lives. The right kind of suffering, he explains, "facing your fate without flinching—is the highest achievement that has been granted to man." Always the clinician, he chose to illustrate this point with a clinical case study and I quote it in its entirety:

A nurse in my department suffered from a tumor which proved to be inoperable. In her despair the nurse asked me to visit her. Our conversation revealed that the cause of her despair was not so much her illness in itself as he incapacity to work. She had loved her profession above all else, and now she could no longer follow it. What should I say? Her situation was really hopeless; nevertheless, I tried to explain to her that to work eight or ten hours per day is no great thing — many people can do that. But to be as eager to work as she was, and so incapable of work, and yet not to despair — that would be an achievement few could attain. And then I asked her: "Are you not being unfair to all those thousands of sick people to whom you have dedicated your life; are you not being unfair to act now as if the life of an incurable invalid were without meaning? If you behave as if the meaning of our life consisted in being able to work so many hours a day, you take away from all sick people the right to live and the justification for their existence." Herein lies the essence of the "will-to-meaning" in Frankl's thought.

The pragmatic realism of Frankl's insight into the meaning of life was one of his most profoundly disarming qualities. He wasn't a romantic nor was he an idealist. He was bluntly realistic about life and the suffering and pain, as well as the joys, which come every individuals way one way or another. "It goes without say," he wrote, "that the realization of attitudinal values, the achievement of meaning through suffering, can take place only when the suffering is unavoidable and inescapable." Suffering and pain is not to be sought; but when encountered, the human person has choices as to how they are to be met. "I have said," Frankl continues, "that man should not ask what he may expect from life, but should rather understand that life expects something from him." Herein lies the essence and genius of logotherapy. The logotherapeutic process, Frankl has argued, is itself educational, educating the individual not simply to look for personal meaning but to explore the meaning which he himself brings to the life situation. "Logotherapy is ultimately education towards responsibility," Frankl wrote, "the patient must push forward independently toward the concrete meaning of his own existence."

In the treatment of the individual, Frankl believed therein was the broader treatment for society at large. No individual is alone in the world and the embracing of one's collectivity with the world, with the social environment of his life situation, is the beginning of mental health. Frankl's concern over the existence of what he called a "collective neurosis" gave way to his belief that the individual's own neurosis, what he called an "existential neurosis," constituted the cure for society at large. Cure the individual's existential neurosis and society's collective neurosis doesn't have a chance. This collective neurosis, which so fascinated Frankl, consisted of four symptoms. First, there was the "planless, day-to-day attitude toward life" which simply indicated that each individual wandered mindlessly through life without direction, hope, or strategy. The dread of war, the overarching fear of global destruction, fosters a kind of do-nothing attitude in the face of this debilitating fear, a gripping kind of anticipatory anxiety which creates helplessness and indolence on the part of a whole society.

Furthermore, beside this absence of motivation and in the wake of no planning, there is the onset of a "fatalistic attitude" toward life. Life has no plan and we are the pawns of fate, helpless to help ourselves. Outside circumstances control the individual and society and there is nothing that can be done to change that. The triumph of a fatalistic worldview, then, gives rise to the third symptom of the collective neurosis, which is "collective thinking" rather than individuated, self-motivated thought. The numbing attraction of the "mindless masses" is strong for those in the grip of the collective neurosis. Man abandons any thought of personal freedom, gives up individual responsibility, and submerges himself into the collective thoughts of the mindless masses. Finally, the collective neurosis produces fanaticism. "While the collectivist ignores his own personality," explains Frankl, "the fanatic ignores that of the other man, the man who thinks differently." The individual and the group alike are possessed by their mindless opinions rather than having and controlling opinions and insights of their own. Group think processes fanaticism and the collective neurosis, then, is in full sway.

It is the "moral conflict," explains Frankl, which produces the cure for the collective neurosis and that cure is what he has chosen to call "existential neurosis." This existential neurosis, an individual rather than collective neurosis, is the product of a moral conflict, a "conflict of conscience." It is the moral conflict itself which serves as a protection for the individual from the symptoms of the collective neurosis, symptoms such as the life without plan or direction, the life of fatalism, of the group think, and fanaticism. "A man who suffers from collective neurosis will overcome it," says Frankl, "if he is enabled once more to hear the voice of conscience and to suffer from it. Existential neurosis will then cure the collective neurosis!"

Within this context, we are reminded of one of Frankl's favorite philosophical statements about the meaning of life, adopted and adapted, ironically, from Frederick Nietzsche. "He who has a WHY to live for can put up with almost any HOW." Throughout his writing and lecturing career, he used this statement over and over again. From his autobiography, he relates a story which captures the essence of his fascination with this statement. Here is a paraphrase of his story as told by Edward Kim. "One night when his fellow prisoners of a concentration camp had received word that they would all be gassed the next day, the people looked to the Viennese psychiatrist for solace. He in turn was able to help each person discover personal reasons to endure which carried them through that dark night with hope and dignity. For example, Frankl helped one person overcome despair by reaffirming the man's fleeting hope that his suffering and death would somehow mean that his wife and family would be saved from such a fate. Instead of perceiving his situation as mere waste and tragedy, this man was enabled to convert his inescapable plight into a noble, heroic deed." Elaborating upon the modified quote from Neitzsche, Frankl says: "a man who becomes conscious of the responsibility he bears toward a human being who affectionately waits for him, or to an unfinished work, will never be able to throw away his life. He knows the 'why' for his existence, and will be able to bear almost any 'how'."

Logotherapy, according to Frankl, "considers man as a being whose main concern consists in fulfilling a meaning and in actualizing values, rather than in the mere gratification and satisfaction of drives and instincts." The nature of being human requires the individual, at all times, to be aware of one's own personal responsibility. The humanizing component of an inhuman experience is the individual's willingness and determination to salvage from the situation an opportunity to serve. "it is life itself that asks questions of man," says Frankl, "It is not up to man to question; rather, he should recognize that he is questioned, questioned by life." Two guiding principles, according to Frankl, direct us to answering the questions of life, namely, conscience and regret. "Live as you were living for the second time and had acted as wrongly the first time as you are about to act now. ... Once an individual really puts himself into this imagined situation, he will instantaneously become conscious of the full gravity of the responsibility that every man bears throughout every moment of his life: the responsibility for what he will make of the next hour, for how he will shape the next day."

THEORIES AND CONCEPTS

According to Frankl, life has meaning under all circumstances, even in the most dire situations. "What matters is not the meaning of life in general," Frankl wrote, "but rather the specific meaning of a person's life at a given moment." Meaning is not "invented" but rather "detected," he points out. We can discover meaning in life, he suggests, in three different ways: (1) by doing a deed; (2) by experiencing a value — nature, a work of art, another person, love, etc., and (3) by suffering. In his autobiography, Frankl's relates a story relative to this third way of finding meaning in life, the way he spent so much time analyzing:

"Once, an elderly general practitioner consulted me because of his severe depression. He could not overcome the loss of his wife who had died two years before and whom he had loved above all else. Now how could I help him? What should I

tell him? I refrained from telling him anything, but instead confronted him with a question, 'What would have happened, Doctor, if you had died first, and your wife would have had to survive you?' 'Oh,' he said, 'for her this would have been terrible; how she would have suffered!' Whereupon I replied, 'You see, Doctor, such a suffering has been spared her, and it is you who have spared her this suffering; but now, you have to pay for it by surviving and mourning her.' He said no word but shook my hand and calmly left the office."

A concept of humanity is held, consciously or not, by every school of psychotherapy. We have seen it in Freud, Adler, and Jung, and so likewise here with Frankl. That "concept of man," says Frankl, affects everything, all conceptual development, all theories of treatment, all clinical perceptions. We must raise this concept of man into the light of day for critical analysis if we ever hope to understand the differences in psychotherapeutic modalities of treatment. "For," says Frankl, "a psychotherapist's concept of man ... can reinforce the patient's neurosis, can be wholly nihilistic." For Frankl, there are three fundamental characteristics of human existence which converge to define the human person, namely, spirituality, freedom, and responsibility. We will here take a closer look at these fundamental characteristics for, according to Frankl, they affect every attempt to understand who we are and what we are to do.

Neither a proponent of religion and religious institutions nor an opponent, Frankl simply intends for spirituality not to be tied up with a specific notion of religion. Where religion helps a person through the day, Frankl has no objection to it. Where religious worldview and ethos stifle, cripple, delude an individual, Frankl is opposed to it. What Frankl means by "spirituality" as a fundamental component of human nature is man's capacity for a sense of awe, wonder, and mystery, even reverence, in one's assessing the experience of life. The connectedness of all things as experienced in moments of high sensitivity or even ecstasy is the role spirituality plays in the human character. A deeply felt sense of beauty and power and wonder in the universe, a hightened experience of integrality, what I have in another place chosen to call "systemic integrality," constitutes what spirituality means in logotherapy. Whether one is a theist, an atheist, or an agnostic, Frankl contends that the dynamics of spirituality can be equally and meaningfully operative within a person's life.

Complimenting spirituality, Frankl suggests, is the characteristics of "freedom." "Freedom means," says he, "freedom in the face of three things: (1) the instincts; (2) inherited disposition; and (3) environment." Frankl engages in a long and definitive discussion of freedom in his little classic, *The Doctor and the Soul*, owing no doubt to his own personal experience with its presence and absence in his trying experiences in captivity. The converging of these three components of instincts, heredity, and environment constitutes the matrix out of which the human experience of freedom can grow and thrive in a person's life. To rise above one's instincts, says Frankl, is a distinctively human possibility and, unlike Freud's obsession with the power of instincts in governing human behavior, Frankl specifically calls upon the responsible person to take his instincts in hand, use them but control them, for service to others. Likewise with heritage, one cannot deny one's own genetic composition but in the acknowledging of it one asserts power over its domination. A determinist, Frankl was most certainly not. He believed in the human person's ability to behave responsibly with self-knowledge. Knowing of one's instincts and one's genetic heritage comes a source of strength and power to control, direct, and utilize the primordial nature of these characteristics for the good of self and humanity. Finally, Frankl was not a member of the "nurture" crowd of behavioral psychologists who would attribute, even blame, one's social and physical environment for the way individuals turn out in their maturity. These three components of freedom, namely, instincts, heritage, and environment, may be used by man to realize freedom if he becomes aware of them, embraces them, and directs them towards a meaningful purpose in life.

Besides spirituality and freedom, however, there is responsibility. Having been greatly influenced in his formative years with the writings of the existentialists, not least being Kierkegaard, Sartre, and Heidegger, Frankl was most insistent that for man to be fully human, he must exercise responsibility. Man is responsible to his own conscience first and foremost, says Frankl. Conscience, says he, is a "thing in itself," it is *sui generis*. It is so fundamental to the human person that humanity cannot exist without it nor the human person remain human without it. Conscience has to do with the drive to do the right thing because it is the right thing to do. This is so fundamental to the human experience that without it humanity and civilization itself could not exist. In his arguments against Freud, Frankl has said. "If we present a man with a concept of man which is not true, we may well corrupt him.

When we present man as an automation of reflexes, as a mind-machine, as a bundle of instincts, as a pawn of drives and reactions, as a mere product of instinct, heredity, and environment, we feed the nihilism to which modern man is, in any case, prone." He believed earnestly that the "ultimate consequences of the theory that man is nothing but the product of heredity and environment" were the gas chambers of Auschwitz. And in speaking of the meaning and function of conscience in the lives of every individual, he wrote: "I am absolutely convinced that the gas chambers of Auschwitz, Treblinka, and Maidanek were ultimately prepared not in some Ministry or other in Berlin, but rather at the desks and in the lecture halls of nihilistic scientists and philosophers." Frankl summed up his assessment of man's capacity for evil this way: "Since Auschwitz we know what man is capable of. And, since Hiroshima, we know what is at stake."

Of the many conceptual contributions Frankl and logotherapy have made to modern psychotherapy, three stand out most conspicuously, namely, tragic triad, existential vacuum, and paradoxical intention. Let us consider each here briefly in concluding our discussion of Frankl and logo-therapy as a classic school of thought.

The tragic triad of human existence is made up of pain, guilt, and death. These are universal human experiences and no one can escape them. An address by logotherapy to the tragic triad should not be perceived as indicative of a pessimistic therapy but rather logotherapy specifically addresses these human experiences to demonstrate how even the most acutely emotional experiences of negativity can be transmogrified into a cause for optimism and hope. Because a fundamental feature of the human spirit is the capacity to change, to redirect oneself, to take on a new outlook on life, the individual can address the realities of pain and guilt and the eventuality of death with a personal sense of empowerment, of responsibility, of courage to face and change the future. We cannot, of course, undo the past but we can, with courage and responsibility, address the present and anticipate the future with hope. We cannot forgo pain but we can address its reality with a sense of fulfilling our life with meaning and purpose in the face of it.

Logotherapy says that our purpose in life is not merely to seek pleasure, as with Freud and the psychoanalysts, but to embrace life with courage and responsibility, to convert meaningless pain and suffering into a purposeful direction by identifying the perimeters of its meaning. Because life is not forever, the human person is under an imperative to utilize the time and talent he has to make a difference in the world. If life were eternal, then we would never have to do anything! Because of the inevitability of our demise, with the clock ticking, with time running out for each individual, we have the responsibility and, indeed, the privilege of finding the meaning of life by addressing the demands of life in service to others. Through the exercise of the will to meaning, meaning is found and life is fulfilled.

The presence of the existential vacuum is rampant in the modern age according to Frankl's assessment. This experiential vacuum has emerged due to two fundamental causes. First, we lost a sense of animal security through the evolution of our species from merely animal instinct to human behavior. Instincts provide a kind of security for behavior is more or less determined. With the coming of reflective self-awareness, that is, consciousness, the human animal shed such instinctual dominance and took on the responsibility of controlling and directing his behavior. With the loss of instincts to guide our behavior, a certain sense of security was lost as well and we became responsible for our own behavior, its consequences and its ramifications.

But furthermore, we also, through time, lose the security which traditions have offered us as mechanisms of security, pointing the way, establishing and maintaining acceptable behavior, and providing perimeters of human social interaction. With the loss of instincts, we must discover or explore and establish modes of conduct, patterns of acceptable behavior, and consequences for failing to conform to the will of the people. When we desire to do what other people do, we call this "conformism." When we do what other people wish us to do, we call this "totali-tarianism." And, finally, when we refuse to follow anyone's direction or guidance in our behavior, we call this "rebellion." The existential vacuum caused by these two losses, instinct and tradition, leads to a neurosis characterized by the four symptoms which we have discussed earlier, namely, (1) a life without direction, (2) a fatalistic view of life, (3) group think, and (4) fanaticism.

Finally, the third major conceptual development in logo-therapeutic theory gave rise to the "paradoxical intention." As is common knowledge in clinical studies of anxiety, the very thing one fears is often the very thing that is produced by that fear. This Frankl has chosen to call "anticipatory anxiety." An example he commonly used to explain this phenomenon is that of insomnia. In such a case, the patient reports that he has trouble getting to sleep. The very fear of not sleeping brings on the thing feared. The same is true of sexual problems such as impotence, the more one thinks about it the more that fear makes it a reality. From this commonly observed clinical situation, logotherapists have developed paradoxical intention as a treatment modality. Frankl tells the story of a young physician who sweated excessively when in the presence of his chief. At other times, he was not bothered by this problem. The patient/physician was advised to resolve deliberately to show the chief just how much he really could sweat. Through this paradoxical intention, he was able to free himself of his problem. The treatment consists not only in a reversal of the patient's attitude towards his problem, whatever it might be, but also that it introduces a level of humor in the process. The logic is simple. Phobias and obsessive-compulsive neuroses are partially due to the increases of anxieties and compulsions caused by the endeavor to avoid or fight them. The subconscious, Frankl points out, cannot tell the difference between a fear and a wish and so attempts to bring either into reality. A phobic person usually tries to avoid the situation in which his anxieties arise, while the obsessive-compulsive tries to suppress and fight his problem. In either case, the result is a strengthening of the symptoms.

More so with Frankl than with any other psycho-therapist considered in this book, personal life story proved to be a major factor in the development of a therapeutic system of theory and practice. Freud's life, Adler's life, and Jung's life, have all proved interesting and have in their own way showed how their life and work were integrated. But with Frankl, it is inconceivable to imagine logotherapy as a school of thought being produced in the absence of his concentration camp experience. The viability of his theory and the utility of his clinical practice both rely upon the life history of its creator. Frankl's relevance to contemporary treatment in therapeutic settings is becoming increasingly recognized and appreciated within a broad spectrum of clinical practice. The impact of his therapeutic system of theory and treatment has yet to reach its maximum level of influence in contemporary counseling circles.

Chapter V

Abraham Maslow
and Humanistic Psychology

BIOGRAPHICAL SKETCH

Abraham Harold Maslow was born in Brooklyn, New York, on the first of April, 1908, the first of seven children to parents who were uneducated Jews from Russia. Pushed hard to succeed by ambitious but misguided parents, he took solace in books from his loneliness and shyness perpetrated somewhat by an extremely aggressive and, as he later said, a schitzophrenic mother. "With my childhood," Maslow wrote late in life, "It's a wonder I'm not psychotic. I was a little Jewish boy in the non-Jewish neighborhood. It was a little like being the first negro enrolled in an all white school. I was isolated and unhappy. I grew up in libraries and among books, without friends." During the summers, he worked for his family's barrel manufacturing company with his three brothers who still own the company. Because he was intellectually gifted, he did find some happiness and a sense of fulfillment during his four years at the Brooklyn Borough High School where he distinguished himself academically.

The study of law, his father's ambition for him, lasted only a few weeks at the City College of New York and he then transferred to Cornell for a few courses but returned to CCNY but failed to complete his degree course. Later in life, he explained that he felt that law dealt too much with evil people and was not sufficiently concerned with the good, and it was the good, the wholesome, the fulfilling experience of a meaningful life that captured his imagination. At the time, Maslow married his high school sweethart who was also his first cousin and, as he put it, his first and last love, Bertha Goodman, a local girl from a good Jewish family and they eventually had two daughters, the experience of which Maslow said changed the direction of his life forever. "Life didn't really start for me," he says, "until I got married and went to Wisconsin." They were married on Christmas Day, 1928, when Maslow was 20 and his bride 19.

Fascinated with the prospects of studying with some of the greatest scholars of the day, Maslow applied to and was accepted at the University of Wisconsin where he earned his B.A. in 1930, his M.A. in 1931, and his Ph.D. in 1934, all in psychology, enjoying the privilege of working with the then famous Professor Harry Harlow. It was his early occupation with behaviorism, from which he later departed with a loud flourish of protestation, and the opportunity of working with Harlow he considered the two driving forces in his academic pursuit of a life's goal as research scholar and teacher. A whirlwind of study, research, writing, and teaching, he had taken Wisconsin by storm and after completing his studies, though somewhat disappointed that he wasn't able, after all, to study with the renown scholars he went to Wisconsin to study with. "I was off to Wisconsin to change the world. But off to Wisconsin because of a lying catalog. I went there to study with Koffka, the psychologist;' Dreisch, the biologist; and Mieklejohn, the philosopher. When I showed upon campus, they weren't there. They had just been visiting professors, but the school put them in the catalog anyway!"

After serving on the Wisconsin faculty as Assistant Instructor in Psychology (1930-1934) and Teaching Fellow in Psychology (1934-1935), Maslow was back to New York in a flash upon graduating with his doctorate specifically to work with E. L. Thorndike as his research assistant at Teacher's College, Columbia University where he became interested specifically in research on human sexuality. At Columbia, he served as a Carnegie Fellow from 1935-1937. His Ph.D. dissertation was an observational study of sexual and dominance characteristics of monkeys! But this study introduced him to a whole new world of research. A full time teaching post was offered him at Brooklyn College and it was during these years, he reflected in older life, that provided him the unparallel opportunity to meet and work with such people ad Adler, Fromm, Horney, and several distinguished Gestalt and Freudian psychologists. Adler, at this time, was holding seminars in his home in New York on Friday nights and Maslow was invited to participate and he always expressed his gratitude for the invitation and the experience. Not inconsequently, he also went through psychoanalysis during this time in Brooklyn. Also, and a world expanding experience it was for him, he served as plant manager of the Maslow Cooperage Corporation, the family factory owned and operated by his three brothers.

He was particularly influenced by two mentors of his during these years, the anthropologist Ruth Benedict and the Freudian psychologist Max Wertheimer. Unlike Freud, Jung, and Adler, Maslow was disinclined to focus his attention and research upon the mentally ill, preferring to study why and how people are mentally healthy, happy, and fulfilled. Eventually, he would develop a whole psychodynamic schema of theoretical constructs and conceptual framework called the hierarchy of needs. Maslow saw needs arranged in a sort of ladder, leading from basic to more advanced levels in the maturation of human fulfillment. It was his becoming a father that seemed to have transformed him into a real force in humanistic psychology. "Our first baby changed me as a psychologist," he wrote, "It made the behaviorism I had been so enthusiastic about look so foolish I could not stomach it anymore ... I'd say that anyone who had a baby couldn't be a behaviorist." His two baby daughters made a profound effect upon him for two reasons. First, because they had such different temperaments, he was forced to assume that many basic personality characteristics were inherited. Second, the birth of his first daughter influenced him to relinquish his belief in behaviorism. He later wrote: "I looked at this tiny, mysterious thing (his first child), and felt so stupid. I was stunned by the mystery and sense of not really being in control. I felt small and weak and feeble before all of this."

Without doubt, it was World War II and the aftermath that changed Maslow forever. It was the defining moment in a research psychologist's life where he turned from behaviorism to humanism and launched a whole new way of thinking about human personality. For him, war epitomized the prejudice, hatred, and baseness of humankind. The experience of witnessing a Victory Day parade, he explains, changed him for good. "As I watched," he recorded years later, "the tears began to run down my face. I felt we didn't understand — not Hitler, nor the Germans, nor Stalin, nor the communists. We didn't understand any of them. I felt that if we could understand, then we could make progress. I had a vision of a peace table, with people sitting around it, talking about human nature and hatred and war and peace and brotherhood ... that moment changed my whole life and determined what I have done since. Since that moment in 1941, I've devoted myself to developing a theory of human nature that could be tested by experiment and research."

From 1951 to 1969, he enjoyed the privilege of teaching at Brandeis University near Boston and for several of those years was department chairman and it was during these fruitful years that he met Kurt Goldstein who planted the seed of an idea in Maslow which gave rise to his now internationally acclaimed concept of "self-actualization." Maslow eventually became the head of what became known as the Third Force in psychology, the humanistic school *vis a vis* Freudian psychology and behaviorism. He ended his teaching carrier by moving to California to become the first Resident Fellow of the w. P. Laughlin Charitable Foundation in Menlo Park. Here he had complete freedom to pursue his interests in the philosophy of democratic politics and ethics but it was here where he died on the 8th of June, 1970, at the age of sixty-two.

Maslow was affiliated, albeit tangentially more often than not, to may professional societies. He served on the Society for the Psychological Study of Social Issues council and was elected president of the Massachusetts State Psychological Association. He presided over the Division of Personality and Social Psychology of the American Psychological Association and was elected president of the APA in 1967. He was the founding editor of both the *Journal of Humanistic Psychology* and the *Journal of Transpersonal Psychology.*

THE CLASSIC TEXT CONSIDERED

Not a prolific writer but one who was able to put his major contributions into a coherent presentation, Maslow established himself as a major figure in American psychology and personality theory with his book, *Towards a Psychology of Being.* "If we wish to help humans to become more fully human," Maslow wrote, "we must realize not only that they try to realize themselves, but that they are also reluctant or afraid or unable to do so. Only by fully appreciating this dialectic between sickness and health can we help to tip the balance in favor of health." In his book, there is a constant optimistic thrust toward a future based on the intrinsic values of humanity. Maslow states that "This inner nature, as much as we know of it so far, seems not to be intrinsically evil, but rather either neutral or positively 'good.' what we call evil behavior appears most often to be a secondary reaction to frustration of that intrinsic nature." He demonstrates that human beings can be loving, noble, and creative, and are capable of pursuing the highest values and aspirations.

Maslow had become disenchanted with classical psychoanalysis and contemporary behaviorism alike for some of the same reasons, primarily because of their intrinsic negativity about the human person and his potential. The first chapter in Maslow's classic is typically entitled, "Toward a psychology of Health." Throughout his career, it was mental health, not illness, that fascinated him, that stirred within him the desire to know more and more about what it means to be human and to grasp the potential of humanity. From within the matrix of this optimism about humanity and our desire to realize our potential grew Maslow's now highly acclaimed fundamental contributions to humanistic psychology, namely, the "hierarchy of human" needs and "self-actualization." then, as we shall see later, his third insight had to do with the emergence of humanistic psychology and what he chose to call the "Third Force."

"There is now emerging over the horizon," he wrote as his opening remarks in this classic text, "a new conception of human sickness and of human health, a psychology that I find so thrilling and so full of wonderful possibilities that I yield to the temptation to present it publicly even before it is checked and confirmed, and before it can be called reliable scientific knowledge." He would not be stopped. The basic assumptions implicit in this new way of thinking about mental health were these: (1) every person has an essential biologically based inner nature, (2) each person's inner nature is in part unique to himself and in part species-linked, (3) this inner nature can be scientifically studied, (4) this inner nature is not intrinsically evil but rather neutral or good, (5) because of this the inner nature should be nurtured and brought out into the light of day, (6) and if this inner core of our fundamental human nature is suppressed or stifled, we get ill, (7) this inner human nature, not like instincts, is frail and in need of much care and attention, (8) and even when suppressed, it endures within the core of human personality, and (9) the nurturing, the fostering, the supporting of these inner nature drives and characteristics inevitably bring mental health.

Toward a Psychology of Being is built upon the humanistic psychology of Maslow's Third Force and constitute the cornerstone of his work. To read this book is to learn of the breadth and depth of the Third Force and to know Maslow at his very core of professional enthusiasm. Its influence continues even today to spread not just throughout the psychotherapeutic community but through the general public, through the humanities, social theory, and pastoral counseling. Its enduring popularity rests with its address to the important questions of the day regarding mental health and the nurture of human potential. Its address to human nature and psychological well-being is a breath of fresh air after the depressing, if not oppressive, nature of classical psychoanalysis and individual psychology which are both built upon the presumption of a "dark closet" needing a good cleaning. Not so with Maslow for his aim is to promote, maintain, and restore mental and emotional health. "Capacities clamor to be used," he wrote, and "cease their clamor only when they are well used ... Not only is it fun to use our capacities, but it is necessary for growth. The unused skill or capacity or organ can become a disease center or else atrophy or disappear, thus diminishing the person."

In this classic, Maslow has put forth a great deal of thought and effort into producing a needs-based framework of human motivation based upon his clinical experiences with humans rather than the behaviorism of Skinner and followers which was fundamentally based upon animal behavior. He was, of course, at odds with Adler, Jung, and Freud as relates to their pessimistic assessment of the human situation for he was both optimistic about human nature and enthusiastic about the development of ways and means of nurturing and fostering human potential and the fulfillment of human aspirations. Many in the fields of management and leadership find Maslow's theory of motivation provocative and stimulating.

The basis of Maslow's theory is that human beings are motivated by unsatisfied needs, and that certain lower factors need to be satisfied before higher needs can be met. We will discuss these in more detail in the "concepts and theories" section but for now let it be said that according to Maslow, there are "general types of needs" such as physiological, survival, safety, love, and esteem, which must be satisfied before an individual can act unselfishly. These he called "deficiency needs" and as long as the human person is being motivated by these drives, we are moving towards growth, toward what he came to call "self-actualization." Satisfying needs, then according to Maslow, is healthy, necessary, beneficial to the individuality, whereas the stifling of this drive to satisfy the fundamental needs lead to mental illness.

Maslow understood human needs to be hierarchical in the sense that one builds upon another like the steps of a ladder or a staircase. The most basic and almost primordial or instinctual needs, he suggests, are air, water, food, and sex. Above those, which must be met in order to progress up the hierarchy, are safety needs such as security and stability and those are followed by more psychologically charged social needs including the need to belong, for love and acceptance. At the upper echelons of the needs ladder are the self-actualizing needs by which Maslow meant the need to fulfill oneself, to realize one's own potential. In order to progress up these stair steps to fulfillment, each level must be realized. There is no "skipping" of the various needs recited here, says Maslow, otherwise, the stifling of these needs at one level precludes full realization at the next level. Not everyone is destined to progress; some never do and thus mental illness is forever a reality. Few reach the highest echelon of self-actualization and Maslow would have us understand that these are not static levels but fluid and fluctuating with time and life circumstances.

The goal, of course, is to reach the highest realms of human potential and that, Maslow calls "self-actualization." The fundamental features of this level of personal growth includes such things as focusing upon the problems outside oneself, others' problems and issues rather than one's own. Also, having a genuine sense of what is true versus the false and phony are features of this level. Being spontaneous and creative while honoring, not mindlessly conforming to social conventions all bespeak the self-actualized person. Maslow enjoyed identifying such individuals within society, particularly within his own social circles. He often used Ruth Benedict as the quintessential example of the truly self-actualized person.

In *Toward a Psychology of Being*, Maslow ventured into the swift and changing waters of "peak experience" as a way of addressing those moments in some people's lives, though not every one, when the most provocative and stimulating experiences of inner ecstasy occurs. These "peak experiences" are, according to Maslow, those profound moments of love, understanding, happiness, rapture, or insight, when a person feels "more whole, alive, self-sufficient and yet a part of the world, more aware of truth, justice, harmony, goodness, and so on." These peak experiences are reserved for the few self-actualized people in society.

Few psychologists of his day questioned whether or not Maslow was really creative and astoundingly original in his thoughts, insights, and manner of presentation. Before Maslow, psychology and psychotherapy seemed to be dominated by the mentally ill and all theorizing focused upon the "cure" for those individuals. Not discounting the need to address the complex issues of mental illness, Maslow and the humanistic orientation of the Third Force movement turned its attention to human potential, to mental health and its nurture and development. Humanistic psychology gave rise to several different therapies, all guided by the idea that people possess the inner resources for growth and health and that the point of therapy is to help remove obstacles to individual's achieving this. Erik Erikson and Carl Rogers become major bearers of this new way of thinking about psychotherapy.

CONCEPTS AND THEORIES

Few would argue that Maslow's lasting contribution to

psychotherapy and personality theory are his three fundamental concepts of (1) the "Third Force," (2) the hierarchy of needs, and (3) self-actualization. All of his other contributions are subsumed within these three insights. Let us look at each of these more closely in our discussion of the fundamental contributions Maslow has made to psychotherapy.

Maslow's theory of personality represents a decided alternative to the two major shaping forces of contemporary psychology evidenced in both behaviorism and in Freudian psychoanalysis. This alternative personality theory construct and treatment modality led Maslow and his compatriots to think of what they were developing as a third way of treating mental health and mental illness. Thus, it became know and first called "The Third Force" by Maslow himself. This humanistic psychology was decidedly developed intentionally as a third and alternative way from behaviorism and psychoanalysis, both perceived to be pessimistic about human nature and rather inclined to think of the human personality as in some way fundamentally flawed by instinctual motivations at the expense of personal health and wholeness.

Maslow's emphasis and that of the Third Force movement was on mental health and ways of fostering that process of fulfillment evidently desired by all human beings. Toward the end of his life, Maslow pointed out that he did not intend to distance himself and his movement from behaviorism and psychoanalysis for each of those schools of thought had a contribution to make in the understanding of mental illness. He felt, rather, that he had embodied the best of both of these viewpoints and had gone beyond them to a psychology of transcendence. Near the end of his life, Maslow became increasing hopeful about fostering this commitment of the profession to a focus upon mental health and wholeness. He envisioned a psychological Utopia in which healthy, self-actualized people would live and work in harmony.

"Humanistic psychology" was a term coined by a group

of psychologists in the 1960s who joined Maslow's movement towards an alternative psychotherapeutic orientation to that of Skinner and the behaviorists and Freud and the psychoanalysts. It was a movement, not a school of thought. Calling themselves the "Third Force," humanistic psychologists shared a wide range of views and certain fundamental conceptions about the nature of the human person and personality development. Embracing the existential philosophy of "life is what you make it" found in Kierkegaard and Sartre, these psychologists found the fundamental tenant of existentialism to be at the core of their own thought and work, namely, the concept of "becoming." A person is never static; he or she is always in the process of becoming something different. Thus, it is the individual's personal responsibility as a free being to realize his own potentialities. Only by actualizing these potentials intrinsic to the human person can a truly authentic life emerge. Requiring more than biological needs and sexual and aggressive instincts, the human person must build upon these towards a higher self-understanding. The process of becoming, of self-actualization, is, they believed, inherent to human nature itself and to stifle that or demean that character is to diminish humanity itself and destroy the person.

The Third Force held certain insights to be endemic to the movement and to their understanding of human potentiality. (1) the individual is an integrated whole and must not be chopped up into component parts but studied, nurtured, and guided as a single entity. (2) They held to the belief that animal research was essentially a waste of time for human psychologists. Self-reflective awareness and a sense of hope towards the future make the human person unique in the animal kingdom and must be studied in terms of these realities. (3) Man's inner nature is essentially good, not evil, and, therefore, the psychotherapeutic agenda is to nurture the inner self of every individual. (4) The human person's own unique potential is to be cherished above all else. This is often perceived to be the most significant concept in humanistic psychology. (5) The emphasis upon psychological health was the reigning principle guiding the development of humanistic psychology and was the guiding principle of the Third Force. Maslow ranted against the notion that the human person is fundamentally demented by instinctual drives. He said that the two other schools of psychological thought did an injustice to the healthy human being's functioning, modes of living, and life's goals. Freud's obsession with the study of neurotic and psychotic individuals came under particular criticism from the Third Force.

Now let us turn again and more closely look at the nature of Maslow's "Hierarchy of Needs." The fundamental idea behind Maslow's hierarchy of needs is that our lowest level of needs must be satisfied or relatively so prior to moving higher up the scale. We are motivated proportionate to the level of needs we have fulfilled and our motivation comes from their fulfillment. Each level has its own integrity and no movement upwards can occur until there is a reasonable satisfaction of the lower level needs. Those who fail to satisfy the lower level needs are doomed to failure in their aspirations for better things and, says Maslow, mental illness awaits those who try it.

We will here explore the major needs categories developed by Maslow when proposing the "hierarchy." They are (1) Physiological Needs, (2) Safety needs, (3) Love and Belongingness Needs, (4) Esteem Needs, and (Self-actualization Needs. Later in their development and with insights gained from the Third Force, Maslow added Aesthetic Needs, Cognitive Needs, and Neurotic Needs to fulfill his attempt at comprehensiveness.

The most fundamental of human needs are the physiological needs without which there is no life. They include food, water, oxygen, maintenance of body temperature, etc. They are essentially the basic needs of all living things. These physiological needs differ from the higher human needs in two important ways. First, they are the only needs that can be completely satisfied or even overly satisfied. Too much food, for example, is always a possibility. A second characteristic peculiar to these physiological needs is their recurring nature. One is recurringly hungry no matter how satisfied one is at any given moment of eating. Hunger always reoccurs.

When once these most basically fundamental needs are being met, one then is motivated to seek safety and its cognates, such as physical security, stability, dependency, protection, and freedom from such threatening forces as illness, fear, anxiety, danger, and chaos. The need for law, order, and structure are also safety needs explains Maslow. Though these are likewise on the lower end of the spectrum with physiological needs, they are indispensable for the further development of the human person. In modern societies, these are routinely met but for children, who are more often than adults conspicuously motivated by these needs, protection from the threats of darkness, animals, strangers, and punishments are most common and motivate the child to seek their removal from their daily lives. Neurotic adults, also, feel relatively unsafe most of the time. These individuals spend much more time and energy than do healthy individuals in seeking to satisfy their needs for safety and reassurance about the world. These individuals, says Maslow, suffer from what he calls "basic anxiety" which comes with the failure to meet the safety needs of the individual.

If physiological and safety needs are commonly and regularly met in modern society, the need for love and belonging has a somewhat different story to tell. Here we find that most of us find ourselves spending a dispro-portionate amount of time addressing this need for love and belonging. Within the needs complex is the need for friendship, the wish for a mate and family, the need to belong to a group, a neighborhood, a political body, or even a nationality. Sexual relations, human contact, and social interaction are all components of this driving need for love. Without love, Maslow explains, a child cannot grow to psychological health. Adults, however, sometimes become proficient at disguising their need for love just as they may also be adept at hiding the fact that their safety is threatened. Adults who have failed to receive love or have failed to develop the capacity to give love often find themselves engaging in self-defeating behavior. They frequently take on such characteristics as cynicism, coldness, aloofness, calloused disregard for interpersonal interaction, all as a protective mechanism, denying themselves the opportunities for securing love thereby. Others go to the opposite extreme and become so outspokenly needy and solicitous as to drive others away, loosing the very thing they sought.

Contrary to the Beatles' song, "Love is all we need," Maslow says not so. Beyond love and belonging and when those needs are being effectively met, the human person reaches higher up the ladder to what is called the "esteem needs" of human experience. With the strength and assurance of the basic needs having been met and with love and belonging well in hand, the human person seeks more, seeks the respect of others as well as self-respect, confidence, competence, and the esteem of others. The esteem needs function, says Maslow, on two levels. The first is reputation, which is the person's perception of the prestige, recognition, or fame he has achieved in the eyes of other people, and second is self-esteem, defined as the person's own feeling of worth and confidence. Esteem needs, then, are bidirectional. One needs the esteem of others and one needs to have esteem for oneself. You really can't have one without the other and maintain mental health. Self-worth must, however, precede esteem of others. When one has self-confidence, self-esteem, and self-worth, one can then begin to develop a sense of reciprocal esteem from the social environment. It cannot, however, work the other way around. Without self-esteem, one cannot experience the esteem of others. When this does occur, mental illness is most commonly the result.

The final and highest level of the hierarchy of needs is that of self-actualization. But it doesn't automatically follow for most people in the world. To have reached the level of esteem needs satisfaction, most people have arrived at their functional level of behavior and do quite well at it throughout their lives. Only a few can even aspire to another higher, but, for those who do, there is a great sense of personal fulfillment, what Maslow calls "self-actualization" which occurs. Only those who embrace what Maslow has called the "B-Values" can make the final step to self-actualization. Those who hold in high respect, says Maslow, such values as truth, beauty, and justice are potentially likely to reach the fullest level of human personal development. We will consider this final step separately and more fully below.

Maslow went on to suggest that there are three more levels of needs beyond self-actualization! As surprising as that might appear, he felt that the aesthetic needs of individuals come after, not before, the self of self-actualization. Not every person and not every culture is particularly susceptible to the aesthetic needs of human development. But, there are individuals who are themselves fulfilled by this need, namely, the need for beauty an aesthetically pleasing experiences. From the artistic displays of Paleolithic man, the human person and the human community has been aware of and appreciative of this need for beauty. Preferences for beauty over ugliness, order or chaos, structure over disarray has characterized the human community from earliest times.

A complimenting balance to the aesthetic needs beyond self-actualization are the cognitive needs. There is that intrinsic curiosity of the human animal, the human person has a desire to know, to understand, to grasp the meaning and purpose and direction of things. This is a fundamental human drive and has characterized the human animal from Paleolithic times. When these needs, the cognitive needs, are stifled, all other needs are potentially threatened because without knowledge, with information, without understanding life becomes problematic! Self-actualization, says Maslow, depends on utilizing fully one's cognitive potentials, though self-actualizing people need not have outstanding inherent intellectual powers. They do, however, need to know and understand what is going on in the world around them. Knowledge brings with it the desire to know more, to theorize, to test hypotheses, or to find out how something works just for the satisfaction of knowing. This is a human compulsion.

Maslow was no superficial optimist and was fully cognizant of the potential for mental illness within any person. When needs are not met, psychological stagnation and pathology often is the result. Maslow introduced the concept of "neurotic needs" to refer to behavior which is not productive, nurturing, and beneficial to human personality. These neurotic needs perpetuate an unhealthy style of life and have no value in the striving for self-actualization. Usually reactive rather than active, they serve as compensation for unsatisfied basic needs. In the absence of safety, for example, a person may have a strong desire to hoard money or property and this motivator is worthless and even destructive to mental health. This, says Maslow, is the indicator of a neurotic need, namely, it fails to contribute to mental health. "Giving a neurotic power seeker all the power he wants does not make him less neurotic, nor is it possible to satiate his neurotic need for power. However much he is fed he still remains hungry (because he's really looking for something else). It makes little difference for ultimate health whether a neurotic need be gratified or frustrated." In therapy, the counseling will seek to determine what need is not being met and assist the client in addressing that issue thereby reducing or displacing the neurotic need caused by the unfulfilled legitimate need of self-actualization.

Finally and in concluding our discussion of Maslow, we must address his major contribution to personality theory called "self-actualization." The development of this concept came about due to Maslow's concentration on mental health rather than mental illness. Adopting the term "self-actualization" from Kurt Goldstein at Columbia University, Maslow went on to develop it into a fully operational concept and focal point of his personality theory. Self-actualization is the highest level of human motivation characterized by full development of all one's capacities.

It is the rare individual, says Maslow, that reaches this level of needs fulfillment in their personality development. First, the individual seeking self-actualization must not be neurotic nor have any psychopathic personalities disorders. Furthermore, the individual must have the "full use and exploitation of talents, capacities, potentialities, etc." These individuals, rare as they are, are the embodiment of all needs fulfillment. They have the capacity to deal with delayed or denied needs for they have a fully understanding of themselves, their capacity to abstain, to do without, to postpone needs gratification without panic or feelings of deprivation. Maslow summed up a thoroughgoing description of just who these individuals really are. "They listen to their own voices; they take responsibility; they are honest, and they work hard. They find out who they are and what they are, not only in terms of their mission in life, but also in terms of the way their feet hurt when they wear such and such a pair of shoes and whether they do or do not like eggplant or stay up all night if they drink too much beer. All this is what the real self means. They find their own biological natures, their congenital natures, which are irreversible or difficult to change.'

In his major work, *Motivation and Personality,* in 1970 and in response to a continual plea for a recitation of the scope of characteristics of the self-actualized person, Maslow listed fifteen quality which characterize this category of person. Let us list them here and in most instances they appear self-explanatory. (1) More efficient perception of reality (they really see things as they are and not as one would like them to be), (2) Acceptance of self, others, and nature (they are realistic in their assessment of themselves, those around them, and the world outside themselves, (3) Spontaneity, simplicity, and naturalness (they are not phonies in their life and work and are eager to respond to situations as they arise, (4) problem-centered (they are quick to recognize problems outside themselves and equally ready to address them), (5) The need for privacy (they are pleased to have social interaction but equally happy to be alone within themselves without having the experience of loneliness), (6) autonomy (they are not demanding of others or the environment around themselves but enjoy the freedom of personal self-satisfaction, (7)Continued freshness of appreciation (theey are those people who are forever able to see the new and different with appreciation and a valuing of each moment and each experience for its own merits, (8) The peak experience (These individuals are the ones who have both the capacity and the reality of entering into a fundamentally ecstatic experience of life through love, art, music, beauty, the challenge of living, etc., with a sense of purpose. Transcendent experiences are not alien to them nor are they frightened by them but rather enjoy the opportunity of living through them to their fruition.), (9) *Gemeinschaftsgefuhl* or social feeling and interest (An Adlerian term which characterizes the self-actualized person in his capacity to commit to the whole community with passion and care and selflessness, (10) Interpersonal relations (they have the gift of focusing upon relationships which nurture and enrich each participant, (11) The democratic character structure (they embody the sense of fair play, what is right for each and everyone, how to make it happen, and how to foster it in others, (12) Creativeness (they experience the joy of creating things, not just writing poetry or music nor simply doing crafts but a thoroughgoing sense of happiness with their own ability to create something new and different which reflects their own interests and values and passion without the need of praise from others for having created it, (13) Philosophical sense of humor (the thoroughgoing capacity to see the humor in life and in interpersonal relationships without cynicism or rancor, (14) Discrimination between means and ends (they have a healthy capacity to determine what is important to be done and how best it might be accomplished without there being the gross contradictions of means and ends issues about what is of value and worthy of effort, (15) Resistance to enculturation (these are the people who can rise above an existential situation and thereby gain a broader, more complete picture of life's situations and, therefore, are not victimized by their own cultural or situational myopia.

A closing word about the actual psychotherapeutic approach of Maslow seems to be a fitting closing statement for all of his work grew out of clinical practice and was designed to serve clinical training and practice to those who joined the Third Force in psychology. Maslow realized that those who need psychotherapy are normally those least likely to seek it out for they have not met their own needs for fulfillment and, thus, seeking help is not in their purview of options to solve their life's problems. Most individuals who come to therapy have difficulty satisfying love and belongingness needs, says Maslow, and therefore psychotherapy is largely an interpersonal process for these individuals, when and if they choose to seek help. Through a nurturing experience with the therapist, the client may gain satisfaction of their need for love and a sense of belonging and thereby gain confidence and a sense of self-worth. This experience gives the client the capacity to establish healthy relationships outside the clinical environment. To bring this about, the therapist himself must be mentally healthy, a situation which does not always exist and, in fact, many times individuals are attracted to clinical psychotherapeutic practice owing to their mental instability. "the aim of Maslovian therapy," explains Jess Feist, "is to free the person from dependency on others so that the natural impulse towards growth and self-actualization can become active." He goes on to point out that psychotherapists, because they are just people, do not have the capacity to operate in a value-free clinical environment. Yet, the mission is to foster the sense within each client of their own quest for wholeness by pointing out ways and nurturing efforts on the part of the client to reach a sense of needs satisfaction, of fulfillment, of eventually self-actualization.

Chapter VI

Erik Erikson
and Developmental Psychology

BIOGRAPHICAL SKETCH

Erik Homburger (Erikson) was born on the 25th of June, 1902, in Frankfurt-am-Main in Germany and died in Harwick, Massachusetts, on May 12, 1994. His mother was a young woman named Karla Abrahamsen from a prominent Jewish family in Copenhagen and his natural father, a Dane named Erik Salomonsen, deserted his mother before Erik was born. At the time of his birth, his mother was "officially" married to a Jewish stockbroker named Waldemar Isidor Salomonsen, and at his birth in Germany, he was registered as Erik Salomonsen. She later trained as a nurse in Karlsruhe and in 1904 married a Jewish physician named Dr. Theodor Homburger who was, at the time, serving as Erik's own pediatrician. In 1909, Erik Salomonsen became Erik Homburger and in 1911 he was officially adopted by his stepfather. Personal identity was an obsession with Erik throughout his childhood and adolescence for at the temple school the children teased him for being "Nordic," owing to his blonde hair and blue eyes, and at public school he was teased for being a Jew.

Upon Erik's eventual arrival and adoption of America as his homeland, having fled Germany with the rise of Nazi proliferation, he changed his surname to Erikson when he took U.S. citizenship. Personal, racial, and religious identify seemed to have pleagued Erickson from his earliest memories and haunted him throughout his childhood, adolescent, and adult life. It has been suggested that possibly this life experience itself was a significant ingredient in leading him to the development of his now famous eight stages of development.

Following public school in Germany where his first love was quite clearly art, Erikson studied at a variety of places in Munich and Florence and eventually arrived at the door of what was then still a newly emerging discipline in psychology, namely, psychoanalysis. It should be pointed out here that Erikson did not ever pursue formalized educational training beyond the high school diploma, relying rather upon his own confidence and insights into the field of which he was most interested. He did attend a "humanistic gymnasium" in Karlsruhe, Germany, where he was not a particularly good student while, nevertheless, doing quite good work in ancient history and art as his records showed. Refusing to heed his step-father's urgings to pursue medicine, Erikson left home to travel across central Europe and within the next year enrolled in an art school and, for a brief time, accepted the fact that even an aspiring artist could near something in an educational setting.

Becoming restless yet again, Erikson left that school and set out for Munich to study at the famous art school, the Dunst-Akademia. Two years thee, he then moved to Florence while generally wandering aimlessly around Italy "soaking up sunshine and visiting art galleries." He later would write that he finally came to realize that "such narcissism obviously could be a young person's downfall unless he found an overweening idea and the stamina to work for it."

In 1927 at the age of twenty-five, Erikson took up a teaching post at an experimental school for wealthy American children living with their parents in Vienna. This school, called the Kinderseminar, was founded to serve the needs of American professionals studying in Vienna to become psychoanalysts and was under the directorship of a psychoanalyst Dorothy Burlingham who was the daughter of the internationally acclaimed

New York jeweler, Charles Tiffany. She was herself a professional trained psychoanalyst and not reluctant to promote this school of thought to all with which she came in contact. Needless to say, the young Erikson fell under her spell from whom not only did he study and learn as well as undergo psychoanalysis but also was profoundly introduced to the Montessori education method and to Anna Freud herself, a lifelong collaborative friend of Dorothy Burlingham. Erikson also and quite naturally was introduced to and welcomed in the Vienna Psychoanalytic Society which was Sigmund Freud's center of teaching and training psychoanalysis to medical professionals and selected layman alike. Besides undergoing psychoanalysis at the hands of Anna Freud herself, Erikson also took the Certificate from the Maria Montessori Teachers Association in Vienna, his own academic credential throughout his whole professional life.

Naturally, young man Erikson was greatly influenced by these heady relationships and professional experiences which, undoubtedly, were instrumental in fostering his passion for analytical studies of childhood maturation. From a most teaching appointment, Erikson managed to squeeze out an incredibly provocative life experience which led to his now famous ideas and theories about human personality development. In 1929, he married Joan Serson, an American teacher and dancer who was at the time a member of Anna Freud's and Dorothy Burlingham's experimental school in Vienna where Erikson himself taught. By 1933, they had two sons and the whole Erikson family then attempted to emigrate to Copenhagen where he had hoped to secure citizenship based upon his natural father's nationality. He had hoped to establish a psychoanalytic practice there, little known in Denmark at the time, but the effort failed and they were forced to look elsewhere to begin again, having feared Hitler's rise to power. That same year he completed a course of study at the Vienna Psychoanalytic Institute.

His enthusiasm for this general field of work and study eventually led him to emigrate to the US in 1933 where he was,

quite fortuitously, provided study and teaching opportunities at
some of America's most distinguished centers of learning
including Harvard, Yale, and the University of California at
Berkeley. Upon his arrival in Boston in 1933, he set up as one of
the very few child psychoanalysts in the country and carried out
research on children at the prestigious Harvard Psychological
Clinic where he enjoyed a close friendship and working
relationship with both Henry Murray and Kurt Lewin. From
1933 to 1935, he enjoyed an appointment as a clinical and
academic Reseaerch Fellow in Psychology in the Department of
Neuropsychiatry at Harvard Medical School. He momentarily
enrolled in a Ph.D. in psychology at Harvard but quickly, within
months, withdrew never again to make such an attempt. From
1936 to 1939, he served under an appointment in the Department
of Psychiatry in the Institute of Human Relations at the Yale
University Medical School where he thoroughly enjoyed
continuing his work and interest in personality development and
cross-cultural studies.

Erikson's early work concentrated primarily upon
psychological testing with special attention to the ways and means
of extending Freudian psychoanalytic theories in relation to the
effect of social and cultural factors upon human development
and personality. He was particularly fascinated with the impact
of these insights upon how society affects childhood and
development. Because of his driving interest in multi-cultural
studies of childhood and society, he became a great student of
cultural anthropology, especially as relates to the study of children
and personality development cross-culturally. As with Maslow,
the works of Margaret Mead and Ruth Benedict proved pivotal
to his own conceptual framework and subsequent theoretical
development in this area. To further deepen his understanding of
cross-culturalism and child development, he journeyed to the
Native American communities of the Oglala Lakota (Sioux) and
the Yurok peoples where he stayed for extended times of
observation, interviews, etc. The richness of these experiences

fed his ambitions in theory and conceptual development while also demonstrating to him some of the apparent deficiencies of Freudian theory as relates to personality development. This encounter with psychoanalytic shortcomings coupled with the richness of his cross-cultural experiences eventually led to his development of what came to be called the "biopsychosocial" perspective on childhood and society.

Eventually migrating with his family to the University of California at Berkeley in 1939, he continued his concentrated efforts in the study of child welfare and personality development and practiced as a clinical psychologist at the San Francisco Veterans Hospital where he treated trauma and mental illness. By 1942, Erikson had risen to the position of professor of psychology at the University of California at Berkeley where he enjoyed assisting Jean MacFarlane in the Child Guidance Study. During the McCarthy era, he moved back to Massachusetts from whence he had come owing to his refusal to sign a loyalty oath which was now being required of all teachers in the State of California. In 1951, he joined a group of mental health professionals at the Austen Riggs Center in Stockbridge, Massachusetts, which was a private residential treatment center for mentally ill young people. He also, and amazingly, continued to maintain a part-time teaching appointment at the Western Psychiatric Institute in Pittsburgh, Pennsylvania while also teaching at the University of Pittsburgh and the Massachusetts Institute of Technology.

From 1951-1960, he taught and worked in New England, but in the summer of 1960, he spent at year at the Center for Advanced Studies of the Behavioral Sciences at Palo Alto, California, and was the next year rewarded by being invited to teach at Harvard University from which he retired in 1970 from his clinical practice but not from his busy schedule of research and writing. He died in Harwick, Massachusetts, on May 12, 1994 and was followed three years later by his Canadian wife, Joan, whom he had met and married while still living and teaching in Vienna. She was herself an academic and particularly fascinated with the study of childhood development and became a major collaborator with Erikson in his research and publications. They had three sons, one of whom was institutionalized as an infant from Down Syndrome, and a daughter. The experience of having a Down Syndrome child almost wrecked their marriage and the pain and suffering, denial and prevarications, to say nothing of the physical and psychological distancing of themselves from this child, Neil, scared the parents and quite decidedly the other children as well. Most biographers do the disservice of failing to mention Neil Erikson in their biographical sketches of Erikson to the detriment of both Down Syndrome research and the Eriksons alike. Neil was institutionalized from the hospital as a newborn and his siblings were simply told that he died at birth.

Later on, the older son was told of Neil's birth and that he was still alive living in an institution but the other children remained in the dark until Neil's death. Joan visited him infrequently and later he was permanently institutionalized in a prestigious public hospital for mentally retarded children. No photos of Neil were ever taken. At forty-one years of age at the time of Neil's birth, Joan blamed herself and was eaten up by the guilt. The marriage suffered severely as Erik continually attempted to close out the reality of Neil's life. When the Eriksons were moving back to New England, they told their other two children of their seven year old brother, Neil, and that he was to be left behind in California. None of the children had ever seen him. The experience of leaving a little brother behind as they moved away frightened the daughter profoundly and parental trust suffered severely as a result. Neil lived to be twenty-two years old and died in 1965 while Erik and Joan were in Europe. They called their son and daughter who were now living back in California and asked them to arrange for the burial of Neil.

Neither parent returned for the funeral or internment of his ashes.

A prolific writer, it has been suggested that all research

and publication subsequent to his first and indisputably his most famous book in 1950, *Childhood and Society*, was merely a continuing commentary on that book. He continued to push his interest in the life cycle (eight stages of development) during which time he introduced the concept of the "identity crisis" within adolescence. A gradual movement away from psychoanalytic theory and practice was seen as he moved closer to the Third Force and humanistic interests within psychological research and writing. This shift was reflected in his subsequent books such as *Young Man Luther* (1958), *Identity and the Life Cycle* (1959), *Insight and Responsibility* (1964), *Identity: Youth and Crisis* (1968), and *Gandhi's Truth* (1970) which won for him the Pulitzer Prize. In 1974, he published *Dimensions of a New Identity*, and with the editorial revisions made by Joan Erikson, his 1982 book, *The Life cycle Completed: A Review*, was republished in 1996 which happily extended the stages of old age within the life cycle model he had developed, thus completing Erikson's major contribution to developmental psychology.

CLASSICAL TEXT CONSIDERED

Many distinguished scholars have established themselves on the strength of one great book such as Frankl and Adler and Rogers, while others wrote and wrote and wrote, leaving behind a library of research and scholarship such as Freud and Jung and Maslow. It can be argued that Erikson's name and reputation was established and secured with the publication of his first book in 1950, *Childhood and Society*. Erikson's fascination with the study of children, their personality development and their maturation, resulted in the writing of his opus text. Here, he elaborated his approach of "triple bookkeeping," as he called it, namely, that understanding a person or behavior involves taking into account somatic factors, social context, and ego development, each in relation to the other. To unpack the somatic aspect of child development, Erikson developed and helpfully expanded Freud's theory of psychosexual development. Erikson chose to explore the power of social context in relation to child-rearing practices and their effects on later personality through some fascinating anthropological and psychoanalytical analysis of the Native Americans, particularly the Sioux and the Yurok cultures.

Though trained by Anna Freud and within the psychoanalytic tradition of Freudian analysis, Erikson was not disinclined to move in his own sphere of thought just as he had chosen not to pursue a traditional university education. Erikson looked at ego development in particular through an analysis of the significance and role of "play," for it was in child's play that he was able to emphasize the need for integration. These three processes, somatic, social, and ego development, are interdependent and that each is both relevant and relative to the other two. This was quite decidedly an advance over traditional Freudian concepts of personality development and child sexuality.

Before we go further in our appreciative assessment of this classic text, let us simply here recite the primary contributions to the understanding of child development which Erikson has brought to the table of psychological discussion. First, he elaborated and modified the theory of psychosexual development as produced by Freud; second, he drew from his own clinical experience in working with ego development among children for his theory construction; and third, he employed anthropological data to emphasize the significance of the social context for child rearing and cultural process for personality development.

A fundamental component of Erikson's theory of ego development is the assumption that the development of the person is marked by a series of stages that are universal to humanity. This was, of course, a very bold claim. The process whereby these stages evolve, he explains, is governed by the "epigenetic principle" of maturation. By this Erikson is asked to explain: "(1) that the human personality in principle develops according

to steps predetermined in the growing person's readiness to be
driven toward, to be aware of, and to interact with, a widening
social radius; and (2) that society, in principle, tends to be so
constituted as to meet and invite this succession of potentialities
for interaction and attempts to safeguard and to encourage the
proper rate and the proper sequence of their enfolding."

In his great classic, Erikson outlines a sequence of eight
separate stages of psychosocial ego development, colloquially,
"the eight stages of man." Far from the speculative mysticism of
Jung and his genetically inherited "archetypes," Erikson is keen
to postulates that these stages are the result of the epigenetic
unfolding of a "ground plan" of personality that is genetically
transmitted, and this is a "universal phenomenon." By epigenetic
(epi means "upon" and genetic means "emergence"), Erikson has
proposed a concept of development which mirrors the notion
that each stage in the life cycle has an optimal time, i.e., "critical
period," in which it is dominant and hence emerges, and that
when all of the stages have matured according to plan, a fully
functioning personality comes into existence.

Going further, Erikson is eager to emphasize that each
psychosocial stage is accompanied by a "crisis," that is, a critical
turning point in the individual's life that arises from physiological
maturation and social demands made upon the person at that stage.
The various components of personality are, in his theory,
determined by the manner in which each of these crises is
resolved. Conflict is a vital and integral part of Erikson's theory,
because growth and expanding inter-personal radius are associated
with increased vulnerability of the ego functions at each stage.
However, it is important to keep in mind that, according to
Erikson, each crisis connotes "not a threat of catastrophe but a
turning point and, therefore, the ontogenetic source of
generational strength and maladjustment."

In a review of Erikson's Childhood and Society over fifty
years ago, the now famous Dr. Eric Berne reviewed his book for
the New York Times. We will quote extensively and casually

from that review to give an idea of the impact Erikson was having on the psychological professional at the time. Berne himself at the time was being established as a major force for what he called "transactional analysis." He was extremely complimentary of Erikson's pioneer spirit in the study and treatment of children as relates to psycho-analytic understanding of ego development. Erikson, Berne points out, early emphasized the importance of early frustrations and leniencies on the development of adult anxieties and actions, believing that while sexual conflict was at the basis of most neuroticism in Freud, the main reason for emotional disturbances in America today lies in the lack of "an emotional integration." This harps back to emotional immaturity caused by a prolonged period of childhood and to certain unique characteristics of American culture and family training. Erikson, of course, and due to his study of cross-cultural childrearing practices, was very cognizant of the fact that personality development is deeply imbedded in the social mores of the child's own culture. This constituted the fundamental starting point of Erikson's monumental work, *Childhood and Society.* In the next section, we will consider some of the major conceptual frameworks and theoretical constructs which were presented in Erikson's entire corpus of research on personality development.

CONCEPTS AND THEORIES

Without doubt, Erikson is one of the leading 20th century psychologists working in the area of personality development, what he called the psychosocial growth of the ego. Interestingly and not particularly to his credit nor benefit, Erikson always insisted that he was not a creative thinker but rather a commentator and, possibly, an elaborator of the psychoanalytic theories of personality development introduced by Freud. He claimed simply to have complimented Freud's work with further investigations of sociological, anthropological, and biological data relevant to personality. In spite of his protestations to the contrary, there are four distinct areas in which Erikson moved away from and beyond Freudian psychoanalytic theory of personality.

First, Erikson shifted the emphasis from the prominence of the id in Freudian theory to the ego which Erikson believed to be the center and basis of human behavior. Called "ego psychology," this shift proposed an understanding of the ego as an "autonomous structure of personality" which follows a course of social-adaptive development that is distinct from but parallels the id and the instincts. Second, Erikson distinguished himself with his emphasis upon the child's relationship to parents and the socio-historical matrix within family life in which each child's ego develops, for good or ill. Third, Erikson's ego development theory covers the entire span of psychological growth and development throughout the individual's life. Freud's theory was woefully brief after adolescence. Finally, there was a great divide between Freud and Erikson when it came to the nature and resolution of psychosexual conflicts within an individual's life. Whereas Freud wish to resolve these issues by delving into the unconscious reservoirs of the adult through dream analysis and word association, Erikson wished to focus upon the adult's capacity to move forward by assessing life's situations and embracing a mode of operation designed to foster healthy living.

The fundamental ingredient in Erikson's theory of ego development is the assumption that the development of the individual is marked by a series of "stages" that are universal to every person throughout the world. The process whereby these stages evolve is governed by the fundamental principle of maturation, what he called the "epigenetic" principle. Erikson points out that this concept means "(1) that the human personality in principle develops according to steps predetermined in the growing person's readiness to be driven toward, to be aware of, and to interact with, a widening social radius; and (2) that society, in principle, tends to be so constituted as to meet and invite this succession of potentialities for interaction and attempts to safeguard and to encourage the proper rate and the proper sequence of their enfolding."

In his highly acclaimed, *Childhood and Society,* Erikson identified and extensively elaborated upon a sequence of eight separate stages of psychosocial ego development, what was usually in shorthand fashion referred to as the "eight stages of man." These eight stages he carefully identified, in his clinical practice and in his laboratory research as the epigenetic unfolding of a "ground plan" of personality that is genetically transmitted. Whereas Jung would have us believe that archetypes are genetically transmitted, Erikson is keen for us to see that the stages of life are genetically transmitted throughout the human species. The fully matured human person arrives on the scene when each of these eight stages have been allowed to mature and function in their own time within the personality of each individual. However, it must be pointed out that Erikson was also eager for us to understand that each stage of development carries with it a "crisis," that is, a critical turning point in the individual's life that arises from physiological maturation and social demands made upon the person at that stage. Each component of the individual's personality develops in relationship to the method in which and the success with which each crisis is met and handled. Conflict, in Erikson's psychosocial theory of development, is crucial and indispensable for healthy development of the ego in each person.

For Erikson, the psychosocial stages of ego develop-ment were chronologically sequenced and each was companioned with a "crisis" component which could work either positively or negatively. Though accused of being "too mechanistic" in his developmental stages, he was insistent throughout his career that these stages were, indeed, sequential, and most definitely universal to the human animal. We will discuss briefly each stage of psychosocial development and its corollary crisis.

Corresponding only somewhat to Freud's "oral stage" of infant development, Erikson's first stage (Infancy) placed "trust" and "mistrust" in juxtaposition to each other with the psychosocial strength gained by the individual to be "hope." He believed that a sense of trust was essentially the cornerstone of a healthy personality. This sense is sometimes thought of as "confidence," and it grows out of an infant's "inner certainty" about the world as a safe, stable place and people as nurturing and reliable. It all stems from the infant's earliest experiences with mother and feeding rituals. Erikson explains: "Mothers, I think, create a sense of trust in their children by that kind of administration which in its quality combines sensitive care of the baby's individual needs and a firm sense of personal trustworthiness within the trusted framework of their culture's life style. This forms the basis in the child for a sense of being 'all right,' of being oneself, and of becoming what other people trust one will become...." The first major psychological crisis for the child wherein mistrust emerges is related to the quality of maternal care which is unreliable, inadequate, and rejecting, thus fostering a psychosocial attitude of fear, suspicion, and apprehension in the infant. Erikson believes that the development of a healthy personality is not just based on the rise of trust versus mistrust in the infant's earliest maternal experiences but rather of the dominance of trust over mistrust. The psychosocial strength gained from this successful manage-ment of trust over mistrust, says he, is the emergence of "hope" in the child's attitudes towards the future and his social relations with others.

By a year and a half, the child is ready to move to the stage of "autonomy versus shame and doubt" and the personality skill to be learned here is that of "will power." As the child gains in neuromuscular maturation, verbalization, and social discrimination, he begins to explore and interact with his environment more independently and the parents are, therefore, confronted with decisions regarding balancing "holding on" with "letting go." The meeting and handling of this psychosocial crisis, both for the child who wants to "let me do it" and the parent who wants to "let me help you," will set in motion wheels of positive or negative development which not only will encourage or stifle autonomy and shame but will both inculcate a sense of "will power" while affecting the earliest stage of life's sense of trust and mistrust. Each stage of ego development is linked to the previous one and a kind of building block phenomenon occurs such that strong ego boosters grow while weak ego boosters stifle personal development. Failure to inculcate and nurture a sense of autonomy in the child, Erikson believes, will instill in the child a sense of shame, something Erkison believes to be akin to "rage turned upon himself" because he has not been allowed to exercise his personal freedom. Shame grows in the personality traits as autonomy is stifled and, thereby, the curtailment of a responsive feeding of the child's "will power." Erikson goes on to say: "Willpower is the unbroken determination to exercise free choice as well as self-restraint in spite of the unavoidable experience of shame, doubt, and a certain rage over being controlled by others. Good will is rooted in the judiciousness of parents guided by their respect for the spirit of the law." Parental guidance at this stage must be firm, Erikson says, but protective of that sense of trust achieved during the previous oral stage. He continues, "Firmness must protect him against the potential anarchy of his as yet untrained sense of discrimination, his inability to hold on and to let go with discretion. As his environment encourages him to 'stand on his own feet,' it must protect him against meaningless and arbitrary experiences of shame and of early doubt."

From trust to autonomy to a sense of "initiative" is the developmental process of the four to five year old child. The resolution of the conflict between initiative and guilt is the final psychosocial experience in the preschool child's personality development, during what Erikson calls the "play age" of childhood from about four years old to the beginning of formal schooling. This resolution of conflict versus guilt produces in the child a deep sense of purpose or, if negatively resolved, the loss of direction and purpose towards the future. "Initiative," explains Erikson, "adds to autonomy the quality of undertaking, planning, and 'attacking' a task for the sake of being on the move, where before self-will, more often than not, inspired acts of defiance or, at any rate, protested independence."

At this time, a child begins to experience the feeling of being a person who actually counts, one who thinks to himself, "I am what I will be." The balancing of this sense of initiative with the experience of guilt is very much dependent upon how parents handle this last pre-school developmental stage in the child's life. Successful develop-ment of this sense of initiative produces what Erikson calls a "goal-directedness" in the child. "The child begins to envisage goals for which his locomotion and cognition have prepared him. The child also begins to think of being big and to identify with people whose work or whose personality he can understand and appreciate. 'Purpose' involves this whole complex of elements." A sense of guilt, on the other hand, is fostered by parents who employ excessive amounts of punishment (verbal or physical) in response to the child's urge to love and be loved. The child's future potential to work productively and achieve self-sufficiency within the context of his or her society's economic system depends markedly upon the ability to master this psychosocial crisis of "purpose" produced by the initiative versus guilt dialectic.

At stage four, the school age years, the child moved to another major level of ego development and personality. This "school age" period covers the years between six to eleven and in classical psychoanalysis is referred to as the "latency period." Here, the industry-versus-inferiority phenomenon appears and the crisis produced by this tension is that of a sense of competency. We have now moved, in the positively developed personality, from trust to autonomy to initiative to industry or, contrariwise, for the negatively developing personality of the child from mistrust, shame, and guilt to a sense of inferiority. Hope, willpower, and purpose as character traits developed in response to the psychosocial crises of each developmental stage now gives rise to what Erikson calls a sense of competency on the part of the healthy child. Erikson has summarized these developmental stages as a movement from "*I am what I am given*" to "*I am what I will*" to "*I am what I can imagine I will be*" to, now at the fourth stage, "*I am what I learn.*" "In school," Erikson explains, "with varying abruptness, play is transformed into work, game into competition and cooperation, and the freedom of imagination into the duty to perform with full attention to the techniques which make imagination communicable, accountable, and applicable to defined tasks." Learning, demonstrating, moving forward in one's capacity to perform, to compete, and to demonstrate ability. The danger at this stage, of course, lies in the potential of failure which will inculcate a sense of inferiority or incompetency. The child's sense of competency and industry is, in modern society, primarily affected by and determined by his educational successes. Yet, cautions Erikson, a genuine sense of industry involves more than simply one's educational achievements and occupational aspirations for it also includes a feeling of being interpersonally competent, the confidence, if you will, that one can exert positive influence on the social world in quest of meaningful individual and social goals. This fundamental strength, namely, competency, is the basis for participation in the social, economic, and political order of one's culture and society.

The fifth stage of ego development falls between childhood and adulthood and is a pivotal period in the development of the individual. Adolescence is that period in a person's development where "ego identity" and "role confusion" come face to face and the resulting psychosocial crisis of "fidelity." This stage in Erikson's developmental scenario is the most well developed in his overall schema. He elaborates on the nature of "ego identity": "The growing and developing youths, faced with this physiological revolution within them, are now primarily concerned with attempts at consolidating their social roles. They are sometimes morbidly, often curiously, preoccupied with what they appear to be in the eyes of others as compared with what they feel they are and with the question of how to connect the earlier cultivated roles and skills with the ideal prototypes of the day ... The sense of ego identity, then, is the accrued confidence that one's ability to maintain inner sameness and continuity (one's ego in the psychological sense) is matched by the sameness and continuity of one's meaning for others." Three fundamental elements characterize ego identity. First, individuals must perceive themselves as having inner sameness and continuity." They are the same person over all. Second, the individual's social milieu must also perceive a sameness and continuity in the individual, so group affirmation is crucial. Third, the adolescent must have gathered confidence in the relationship between his world and that of his social group by having a sense of who he is and having that affirmed by others. However, when this mutuality of ego identity affirmation is absent, adolescents will encounter what Erikson calls "role confusion." In the absence of a personal identity which is strong enough to see a youngster through these developmental years, an identity crisis is inevitable and Erikson calls this crisis "role confusion." This crisis is most often characterized by an inability to select a career or pursue further education with the added deficit of a deep sense of futility, personal disorganization, and aimlessness. The feeling of inadequacy, depersonalization, alienation, and even a negative identity may result. When the adolescent has confronted the challenge and ego identity has finally emerged sound and operational, "fidelity" emerges and this, says Erikson, refers to the individual's "ability to sustain loyalties freely pledged in spite of the inevitable contradictions of value systems." Being true to one's own will worked out ego identity and remaining loyal to the social matrix within which that ego identity has developed and emerged is a characteristic of fidelity and prepares the adolescent for the next stage of development.

By virtue of the establishment of a well established ego identity characterized by fidelity or loyalty to oneself and one's social milieu, the individual, says Erikson, is now "ready for intimacy, that is, the capacity to commit himself to concrete affiliations and partnerships and to develop ethical strength to abide by such commitments, even though they may call for significant sacrifices and compromises." This is the stage in which courtship, marriage, and early family life come on the scene. By "intimacy," Erikson has in mind the sense of intimacy most of us share with a spouse, friends, brothers and sisters, and parents or other relatives. He also, however, speaks of intimacy with oneself, that is, the ability to "fuse your identity with somebody else's without fear that you're going to lose something yourself." This two pronged sense of intimacy is crucial in a well developed relationship — intimacy with others within the framework of intimacy with oneself. The inevitable danger in this developing sense of intimacy is, of course, is a sense of isolation where neither intimacy nor social involvement is possible or productive. The inability to enter into positive and intimate personal relationships leads the individual to feelings of social emptiness and isolation. Merely formalized and superficial social relationships are inadequate to meet the developmental needs of these individuals, however, and given the fact that they may be suffering from an over dependence upon self-absorbing behavior to relieve their sense of loneliness, they drift further and further away from realistic opportunities to experience and nurture feelings of intimacy. Their behavior, then, becomes inevitably counterproductive.

The psychosocial strength being sought here and the one which is realized in the healthy development of a sense of intimacy is that of love. In addition to its romantic and erotic qualities, Erikson regards love as the ability to commit oneself to others and abide by such commitments, even though they may require self-denial and compromise. "Love," explains Erikson, "is mutuality of devotion forever subduing the antagonisms inherent in divided function."

The "middle years" of an individual's stages of life are fraught with prospects of creative activity or degenerative stifling.

What is not possible is for nothing to happen to the individual's ego development and psychosocial maturation. This process continues throughout life, it does not stop for age and only ends with death. The countervailing options for the middle years adult is either what Erikson calls "generativity" or "stagnation" and the psychosocial crisis product is that of "care."

"Generativity" occurs, says Erikson, when an individual beings to show concern not only for the welfare of the next generation but also for the nature of the society in which that generation will live and work. This developmental stage in life has to do with the willingness, or not, of the individual to meet the challenge of assuming responsibility for the continuation and betterment of whatever is instrumental to the maintenance and enhancement of the society in which the individual lives. It represents the older generation's concern in establishing and guiding those who will replace them. Failure to assume this responsibility, the assert oneself into the mainstream of social betterment and improvement leads to individual and societal stagnation. The sense that one does not wish to be involved, not participate in teaching the next generation the values necessary for successful and fulfilled living, all lead to a failure of courage and a diminishment of one's social worth and the worth of society at large. Those in their middle years who embrace and nurture generativity will produce a sense of "care" needed for the ongoing contribution to the improving quality of life for the next generation. Individuals lacking generativity cease to function as productive members of society, live only to satisfy their needs, and are interpersonally impoverished. This is often called the "crisis of middle age" where the person has a sense of hopelessness and tends to feel that life is meaningless. Caring for oneself, for others, for society at large is the benefit and reward to those who develop and nurture a sense of contribution to the wider society.

The "mature years" constitutes the last stage in life's journey. Every culture has this stage well developed according to its own social values, history, and composition. It is a time when the individual's ego is confronted with the option of "integrity" or "despair" and the crisis which comes with this confrontation can lead to a general sense of "wisdom" about life and how to live it. "Only in him who in some way has taken care of things and people," says Erikson, "and who has adapted himself to the triumphs and disappointments adherent to being, the originator of others or the generator of products and ideas — only in him may gradually ripen the fruit of these seven stages — I know no better word for it than ego integrity." With the inevitable demands brought on by these declining years of the need to adjust to deterioration of physical strength and health, to retirement and reduced income, to the death of a spouse and close friends, and the need to establish new affiliations with one's age group, there is a marked demand for shifting one's attention from a focus upon future life to that of one's past life.

The sharing of past experiences, of days gone by, with those who are younger characterize this stage in life and often, depending on the culture, is perceived by the listeners and observers of these older persons as a sense of "wisdom," a kind of helpful knowledge about what is important and how to live a meaningful and fulfilled life. "The wisdom of old age," explains Erikson, "involves an awareness of the relativity of all knowledge acquired in one lifetime in one historical period. Wisdom is a detached and yet active concern with life in the face of death." On the other hand, the lack or loss of ego integration in older individuals is earmarked by a hidden dread of death, a feeling of irrevocable failure, and an incessant preoccupation with that might have been." "Fate," he explains, "is not accepted as the frame of life, death not as its finite boundary. Despair indicates that time is too short for alternate roads to integrity: this is why the old try to "doctor" their memories." Ego integration leads to a sense of real and practical wisdom worthy to be shared with the young and in that process the individual comes to a deeper sense of self-fulfillment and contentment with life as he has lived it with hope for the future.

Though a trained and never rebellious psychoanalyst in the true Freudian school of thought, Erikson nevertheless never ceased to claim allegiance to Freud and boldly asserted the further development and contribution of his thought to the Freudian school of psychotherapy. His psychosocial theory of personality development relied upon a strong argument for the centrality of ego psychology, developmental changes throughout the life cycle, and an understanding of personality against the background of social and historical forces. Contrary to Freud, Erikson held that the ego was an autonomous personality structure and he concentrated his efforts, therefore, upon ego qualities that emerge during the fundamental stages of maturation.

Erikson argued that the ego continued its develop-ment throughout life and identified eight stages in which that development occurs. These psychosocial stages characterize the human life cycle, as he called it, and he contended that the individual's personality is determined by the resolutions of the conflicts which emerge in each of these developmental stages. His theory is, of course, rooted in his basic assumptions concerning human nature itself, namely, (1) a strong commitment to the assumptions of holism and environmentalism, and (2) a moderate commitment to the assumptions of determinism, rationality, objectivity, pro-activity, heterostasis, and knowability.

Though some have registered concern over the relationship between the personal life of Erikson, his family life and his failure to come to both an emotional and professional embracing of the life of his mentally retarded child, and the profundity of his thought, most psycho-therapists today are indebted to Erikson for calling attention to the eight stages of the life cycle. Granted, they are mechanistic, sometimes even antiseptic, they have, nevertheless, spawned a whole new way of viewing human maturation and have nurtured a deeper appreciation for what a modified psychoanalytic theory of personality can still offer to the modern practice of psychotherapy.

Chapter VII

Carl Rogers
and Person-Centered Psychotherapy

BIOGRAPHICAL SKETCH

The fourth of six children, Carl Ransom Rogers was born on the 8th of January, 1902, in Oak Park, Illinois. His father, Walter Alexander Rogers, was a civil engineer and his mother, Julia Cushing Rogers, a devout Christian woman and traditional housewife. His father held both a degree in engineering and some advanced graduate training as well, all from the University of Wisconsin and his mother had completed two years of college before she married Walter. In his closing years of life, Carl described his parents as "down to earth individuals" but "rather anti-intellectual, with some of the contempt of the practical person toward the long-haired egg-head." Carl was the fourth child and third son but nearly six years later he had two more brothers, Walter and John, who were born in 1907 and 1908 respectively. His oldest brother Lester and his sister Margaret were nearly nine and seven years his senior and he found himself closest emotionally to his younger two brothers. Because Carl was both obviously a gifted child and could read before entering public school, he began in the second grade, and one of his classmates was Ernest Hemingway as well as the children of Frank Lloyd Wright. At the age of twelve years old and owing to the financial success of his father's career, the family relocated to a farm about an hour west of Chicago and for the remainder of Carl's adolescent years, they all remained there.

Life was hard for a city-born boy moved abruptly to the country where farm chores were difficult and demanding, discharged within the strict spirit of an aggressive Protestant ethos and worldview. He believed that his parents were masters of the art of subtle control for he wrote, "I do not remember ever being given a direct command on an important subject, yet such was the unity of our family that it was understood by all that we did not dance, play cards, attend movies, smoke, drink, or show any sexual interest." Little encouragement was given for free time, day dreaming, and child's play and, in the face of such a restricted life, Carl became somewhat introverted, isolated from his fantasy world, independent of spirit, however, and quite decidedly self-disciplined.

Rogers often spoke of his boyhood in less than glowing terms for, says he, they were years of structured, strict, and uncompromising religious and ethical standards dominated by devotion to a fundamentalist kind of faith. "I think the attitudes toward persons outside our large family," he wrote, "can be summed up schematically in this way: Other persons behave in dubious ways which we do not approve in our family. Many of them play cards, go to movies, smoke, drink, and engage in other activities — some unmentionable. So the best thing to do is to be tolerant of them, since they may not know better, and to keep away from any close communication with them and live your life within the family." This uppity condescension characterized the family and, unfortunately, too often characterized his own behavior. In speaking of his high school years, he wrote: "I made no lasting associations or friendships. I was a good student and never had any difficulty with the work. Neither did I have problems in getting along with the other students so far as I can recall. It is simply that I knew them only in a very surface fashion and felt decidedly different and alone, but this was compensated for by the fact that my brother and I went together much of this time and there was always the family at home."

It was to the University of Wisconsin, in 1924, that Carl

was sent to pursue a mixed bag of interests. Both his parents and three of his siblings had attended the University of Wisconsin and an alternative school was never seriously contemplated. Beginning, typically, as an agriculture major with youthful plans of becoming a successful farmer, he drifted towards history, then religion for what he thought would be the ministry, and then, eventually and finally, he took up a serious and sustained interest in clinical psychology. Of course, the University of Wisconsin was just the right place to be to study clinical psychology for it was becoming rather quickly the leading center in the mid-west for that discipline. He always professed to believing that the discovery of psychology constituted the fundamental turning point in his life.

This turning point came during his third year at the University when he was chosen to go to Peking for the "world Student Christian Federation Conference" for the purpose of "evangelizing the world for Christ in this generation!" He wrote later, "I consider this a time when I achieved my psychological independence. In major ways I for the first time emancipated myself from the religious thinking of my parents, and realized that I could not go along with them." He recounts a particularly insightful moment while on board ship returning from the Peking evangelism trip. One evening, aboard ship, a traveling companion, Dr. Henry Sharman, a student of the sayings of Jesus, made some provocative remarks. "It struck me in my cabin," Rogers later wrote, "that Jesus was a man like other men — not divine! As this idea formed and took root, it became obvious to me that I could never in any emotional sense return home." The major result of this trip to Peking and this new insight into his own faith-based self-understanding was that he developed a duodenal ulcer. "Something of the gently suppressive family atmosphere," he mused, "is perhaps indicated by the fact that three of six children in our family developed ulcers at some period in their lives. I had the dubious distinction of acquiring mine at the earliest age."

Though he earned his B.A. in history from the University of Wisconsin in 1924, he had actually only taken one course in psychology and that by correspondence. In 1924, he married Helen Elliot, a childhood sweetheart, and they soon thereafter moved to New York City where he pursued a master's degree from Columbia University while simultaneously attending the Union Theological Seminary, a bastion of liberalism in the 1920s and 1930s. He and Hellen eventually had two children, a boy and a girl. At the seminary, he took a course on the pursuit of the ministry, the nature of the career, its demands and expectations, and during this time he decided, against his parents wishes and expectations, to transfer to psychology at the Teachers College of Columbia University in 1926 and where, in 1927, he won a fellowship to work in the Institute of Child Guidance. At the Institute he gained an elementary knowledge of Freudian psychoanalysis, but was not much influenced by it as his later theoretical work demonstrated. At the Institute he also attended a lecture by Alfred Adler who shocked Rogers and the other staff members with his contention that an elaborate case history was unnecessary for psychotherapy.

Rogers subsequently took from there a masters in psychology in 1928 and a doctorate in psychotherapy in 1931. He was enthralled with clinical work and had already commenced his lifelong career in this field at the Rochester Society for the Prevention of Cruelty to Children. There, he studied Otto Rank's theory and therapy techniques and that experience drove him to believe that he himself could develop operational theories and technique unique to his insights and experience. For the next ten years, Rogers applied himself to psychological services for delinquent and underprivileged children.

At the age of thirty-eight, Rogers received an appointment as "full professor of psychology" at Ohio State University. Despite his fondness for teaching he might have turned down the offer if his wife, Helen, had not urged him to accept and if the University had not agreed to start him at the top, with the academic rank of full professor. He often told his younger students and colleagues that the only way to enter the academy was to do so as full professor. Anything less was not acceptable as it required too much work in areas of no particular interest to the young professor but necessary in order for him to prove himself worthy of the appointment. A major breakthrough in his own self-understanding occurred quite surprisingly in response to a lecture he was invited to give to the Psi Chi chapter at the University of Minnesota. The lecture, entitled, "Newer Concepts in Psychotherapy," raised such furor and controversy at the lecture that it occurred to him that he was saying something quite new and provocative. This lecture became the backbone of the second chapter in his new blockbuster book, *Client-Centered Therapy,* published in 1942.

From 1940 to 1945, he taught psychology and, in 1942, his published his first of several major books. This one, entitled, *Counseling and Psychotherapy: Newer Concepts in Practice,* was the first of its kind in the profession of psychological counseling where the psy-chologist's clinical results based upon the recording and transcript of the client's therapy session were used for analysis in print. He set a precedent and the profession burst upon the scene with therapy-session based clinical reports and analyses like it had never done before. His publishing became prolific in the journals as a result of this new method of presenting psychological data.

After five years of teaching at Ohio State, Rogers took a one year appointment in 1944 in New York as Director of counseling Services for the United Service Organization. Rogers was subsequently offered a post at the Counseling Centre of the University of Chicago where he served from 1945 to 1957 and where he wrote, in 1951, the most important book of his career, entitled, *Client-Centered Therapy: Its Current Practice, Implications, and Theory.* The groundbreaking nature of this book's fundamental theories about counseling would change the face of that profession forever and would catapult Rogers into international acclaim. That same year and thanks to the notoriety of the book, he was appointed head of the Counseling Center at the University of Chicago. At the time, the famous Dr. C. George Boeree made this following assessment: "Rogers' theory is particularly simple — elegant even! The entire theory is built on a single 'force of life' he calls the actualizing tendency. It can be defined as the built-in motivation present in every life-form to develop its potentials to the fullest extent possible. We're not just talking about survival: Rogers believes that all creatures strive to make the very best of their existence. If they fail to do so, it is not for a lack of desire."

Though his six years at the University were outstandingly successful, he left in 1957 to take up a joint post at the University of Wisconsin as both Professor of Psychology and Professor of Psychiatry. He stayed, however, only two years for he found that he was becoming disillusioned with the therapeutic and diagnostic techniques of the establishment at the time particularly in the psychopharmacologically-driven department of psychiatry as well as with the overall pedagogical philosophy of the graduate program generally. So, in 1959, he joined the Western Behavioral Sciences Institute in La Jolla, California. In 1961, he wrote what has become his most internationally recognized published, *On Becoming a Person*. During the years 1962-1963, he was a Fellow at the Center for Advanced Study in the Behavioral Sciences at Stanford University. He concentration was on group social relations, and by 1968, he had a handful of colleagues who chose to separate from the Institute and found their own, known as the Center for the Studies of the Person, based in La Jolla as well. A summary report indicated that, "...subsequently, throughout the 1960s and 1970s, Rogers spearheaded the development of personal-growth groups, and his influence spread to working with couples and families; and his ideas were also applied to administration, minority groups, interracial and intercultural groups, and international relationships." At the Center, he continued to provide therapy for select individuals and couples, and was prolific in his research and writing. In 1987, having broken his hip, he died in surgery on the 4th of February.

Rogers early on avoided the development of a theory of personality but eventually, from peer pressure, he worked on his theory of personality which became a core of all of his writings. First expressed in sketchy form in his 1947 Presidential address given at the American Psychological Association, he further developed it in his great classic, *Client-Center Therapy* in 1951 and eventually fully developed in his greatest work of all, *On Becoming a Person.* Nevertheless, he was always insistent that the theory should remain tentative. It is with this thought that one must approach any discussion of Rogerian personality theory.

Carl Rogers was honored the world over and towards the end of his life was nominated for the Nobel Peace Prize for his work with national inter-group conflict in South Africa and Northern Ireland. He had received countless honorary degrees from distinguished international institutions such as the University of Santa Clara, Gonzaga University, the University of Cincinnati, and Northwestern University as well as a Doctor of Philosophy degree from the University of Hamburg in Germany and the Doctor of Science degree from the University of Leiden. As early as 1944, he was president of the American Association for Applied Psychology and two years later the presidency of the American Psychological Association. In 1956, he became the first president of the American Academy of Psychotherapists and in 1964 was selected as the Humanist of the year by the American Humanist Association. We can close this biographical sketch with the citation given to Rogers by the American Psychological Association when, in 1972, they awarded him the coveted Distinguished Professional Contribution Award. It reads:

"His commitment to the whole person has been an example which has guided and challenged the practice of psychology in the schools, in industry, and throughout the community. By devising, practicing, evaluating, and teaching a method of psychotherapy and counseling which reaches to the very roots of human potentiality and individuality, he has caused all psychotherapists to re-examine their procedures in a new light. Innovator in personality research, pioneer in the encounter movement, and a respected gadfly of organized psychology, he has made a lasting impression on the profession of psychology."

CLASSIC TEXT CONSIDERED

Some psychotherapists we have considered in this study established their reputation on one major book. Others wrote numerous books to establish themselves. Rogers, though he wrote much and often, established himself on the basis of two major works, namely, *Client-Centered Therapy* (1950) and *On Becoming a Person* (1961). Roger's first and overriding characteristic in the writing of his first major book was to emphasize the warmth and acceptance of the counseling relationship between the counselor and the client or patient. His first major book was meant to emphasize the new rationale of his approach, namely, "The client, as the term has acquired its meaning, is one who comes actively and voluntarily to gain help on a problem, but without any notion of surrendering his own responsibility for the situation."

From non-directive counseling to client-centered counseling to, finally, person-to-person therapy, Rogers' thought has continued to grow and expand. Yet, his initial entry into the cauldron of psychotherapeutic theorizing in his first book (1950) to his major opus of 1961 finally culminating in his late work all bespeak of capacity to grow through learning in the clinical environment. He gradually came to realize that the relationship between therapist and client is the most important aspect underlying personality change. Herein lay his interest and this is where he concentrated the bulk of his entire career.

Rogers brought to the psychotherapeutic table a new way of seeing the counselor's role in relationship to the client. He suggested that the emphasis shift from an objectified standoffish posture to an "empathic" approach in understanding the client's world, and then to seek to "communicate" that understanding directly to the client. In mirroring back to the client's the feelings the counselor pick up on in the interview encounter, the counselor simul-taneously transmitted the desire to perceive the world as the client perceived it, thus, the role of "non-directivity" in the dyadic relationship. Rogers insisted that the counselor's role was to achieve an "internal frame-of-reference" with the client. "It is the counselor's aim," says Rogers, "to perceive as sensitively and accurately as possible all of the perceptual field as it is being experienced by the client ... and having thus perceived this internal frame of reference of the other as completely as possible, to indicate to the client the extent to which he is seeming through the client's eyes."

In the "new" psychotherapy, Rogers emphasized four important principles. First, the new therapy "relies much more heavily on the individual drive toward growth, health, and adjustment. Therapy is not a matter of doing something to the individual, or of inducing him to do something about himself. It is instead a matter of freeing him for normal growth and development." Second, "this new therapy places greater stress upon the emotional elements, the feelings aspects of the situation, than upon the intellectual aspects." Third, "this new therapy places grater stress upon the immediate situation than upon the individual's past." And, fourth, this new approach "lays great stress upon the therapeutic relationship itself as a growth experience.

Here the individual learns to understand himself; to make significant independent choices, to relate himself successfully to another person in a more adult fashion." Rogers firmly believed that individual by and large had it within themselves to solve their own problems. The task, then, of the therapist, in Rogers' view, was to establish the conditions which would allow individuals to attain this insight for themselves. "Attainment of insight" was, therefore, one of the key goals of nondirective therapy. On the other hand, the counselor's chief task was to reach the "clarification of feelings" through rephrasing the emotional content of the client's statements such that the client gained a new insight into his own stated condition. "Effective counseling," says Rogers, "consists of a definitively struc-tured, permissive relationship which allows the client to gain an understanding of himself to a degree which enables him to take positive steps in the light of his new orientation."

The three major elements characterizing Rogers' theory of personality were (1) the necessity for the counselor to provide a warm and permission relationship for the client, (2) the necessity for the counselor to assume the internal frame of reference of the client and to communicate empathic understanding of the client's world, and (3) finally, to reach a mutual expression of feelings between the client and the counselor thereby realizing the full potential of the client-centered theory of personality and psychotherapeutic treatment.

Rogers identified six conditions of client-counselor relationships which, if met, would constitute the basis for a successful therapy. He believed he had already proven clinically that a theoretical rationale for personality change in therapy was possible which implied that constructive alterations in personality could occur regardless of the specific verbal techniques employed by the counselor. He recited these six conditions to reinforce his theory. First, two persons are in psychological contact such that each of them is fully aware that the other's presence makes a difference. Second, the client is in a state of incongruence in relationship with the counselor due to a "discrepancy" between the client's self-image and his existential experience in the counseling environment. Third, the therapist is, on the other hand, congruent (which means integrated) in the relationship due to the pre-set definition of his role in the situation. Fourth, the therapist experiences unconditional positive regard for the client as this is crucial in order to establish a report in the counseling milieu. Fifth, the therapist experiences an empathic understanding of the client's internal frame of reference and endeavors to communicate this experience to the client such that the encounter proves therapeutically successful in direct correlation to the therapist's capacity to emote empathy. And, sixth and finally, the communication to the client of the therapist's empathic understanding and unconditional positive regard must be minimally achieved or, otherwise, no helpful therapeutic result will occur.

CONCEPTS AND THEORIES

Rogers was a conspicuous member of the Third Force, the humanistic psychological school which set itself along side but *vis a vis* both psychoanalysis and behaviorism. His understanding of human nature was, of course, central to his position as a leader in the Third Force movement. He speaks of the driving force in his work which is "the continuing clinical experience with individuals who perceive themselves, or are perceived by others to be, in need of personal help. Since 1928, for a period now approaching thirty years (he wrote in 1958), I have spent probably an average of 15 to 20 hours per week, except during vacation periods, in endeavoring to understand and be of therapeutic help to these individuals. From these hours, and from my relationships with these people, I have drawn most of whatever insight I possess into the meaning of therapy, the dynamics of interpersonal relationships, and the structure and function of personality." Rogers firmly believed that at the core, every human being is fundamentally good, being essentially purposive, forward-moving, constructive, realistic, and trustworthy. Because of this essential goodness of the human person, every individual given the right opportunity for growth, love, and affirmation will blossom forth in his own innate potential, optimum personal development and effectiveness.

Christianity, he argued, has nurtured a core belief in the innate evil of the human person, an inclination to evil and sin. Furthermore, he is unabashed in arguing that this demented notion of human nature has been influenced, even trumped, by Freud and the psychoanalytic school of psychotherapy. If permitted to run free from the scrutiny and domination of the ego and the superego, the human personality's id and unconscious would manifest itself, according to Freud and Christians, in incest, homicide, thievery, rape, and other horrendous acts of self-destructive behavior. People do engage in such behavior and this occurs when they have been stifled, been misdirected, or their natural personality development has been suppressed from its natural inclinations. When, however, people are able to function as "fully human beings," when they are free to experience and express themselves, they show a positive and rational approach to life which elicits trust and nurtures harmony in interpersonal relationships.

Rogers protested against those cynical and jaded psychotherapists who thought of him as naïve and simplistic: "I do not have a Pollyanna view of human nature," he argued. "I am quite aware that out of defensiveness and inner fear individuals can and do behave in ways which are incredibly cruel, horribly destructive, immature, regressive, anti-social, and harmful. Yet, one of the most refreshing and invigorating parts of my experience is to work with such individuals and to discover the strongly positive directional tendencies which exist in them, as in all of us, at the deepest levels." This driving force in human nature towards the good and self-fulfilling he calls the "actualizing tendency," and he believes it is latent in every human being. He defines it as "the inherent tendency of the organism (the personality) to develop all its capacities in ways which serve to maintain or enhance the person." Therefore, says he, the fundamental principle guiding every person's life is the drive to actualize, maintain, or enhance themselves, indeed, to become the best that their inherited natures will permit them to be. This is, essentially, the sole motivating principle in Roger's theory of personality.

To be sure, there are certain definitive characteristics which establish this actualizing tendency. Let us explore them momentarily here. Of course and to begin with, says Rogers, there is a "biological factor" which is operative here, namely, this tendency is an inborn characteristic necessary to maintain the individual but also for the enhancement of the individual by providing a mechanism for the development and differentiation of the body's functions, growth, and development. But, of more importance than even this is the motivating force which the actualizing tendency provides for in increased autonomy and self-reliance in pursuit of the individual's full potential in life. Furthermore, the actualizing tendency is mot merely for the reduction of tension in the stresses of one's physical or biological life, contrary to Freud's insistence on the prominence of instincts. Rather, the individual is motivated, says Rogers, by a growth process in which potentialities and capacities are brought to realization. This actualizing tendency, then, says he, "is the essence of life itself."

The actualizing tendency, explains Rogers, serves as a criterion against which all of one's life experiences are evaluated and, particularly, when individuals engage in what he calls the "organism valuing process." This process involves the individual's overt effort in maintaining and enhancing the sought after and valued positive behaviors and experiences in life for they produce within the individual a strong feeling of satisfaction in the realization of one's full potential. This "process" is a mechanism for the evaluation, the weighing, the determining whether or not an experience is affirmative or negative to self-fulfillment. And, the most critical aspect of this actualizing tendency, says Rogers, is the individual's drive toward self-actualization, what he has called the "self-actualizing tendency." This particular tendency, then, is what gives a forward thrust to life, to the individual who must encounter and incorporate life's complexities, self-sufficiency, and maturity. "Self-actualization," then, is the process of becoming a more adequate person.

Rogers counted himself among the phenomenologist of the day who were practicing humanistic psychology as members of the Third Force. The Third Force was never a formal body but consisted of humanistic psychologists who pushed their worldview as a viable alternative to Freud and Skinner, or psychoanalysis and behaviorism, in both theory and practice. Phenomenological psychology contends that the "psychological reality" of the individual's world is exclusively a function of the way in which the world is perceived by that individual. The truth doesn't really matter because it can never really be identified. What really matters to the individual is what that person thinks is true, sees to be true, acts in relationship to what he sees and thinks to be the truth. Phenomenological psychology argues that what is real to an individual, that is, what reality is thought, understood, or felt to be, is that which exists within that person's "internal frame of reference." It is this frame of reference which is important in the psychotherapeutic relationship. Rogers was insistent upon this point, namely, that every individual interprets his world and that interpretation is what the therapist must come to grips with. The only way to "understand" an individual's behavior and attitude is to come to an understanding of this internal frame of reference. It is the "subjective reality" of the client's perceived world which is important, not the objective truth.

Needless to say, Rogers' identification with the phenomenological approach to personality theory is based upon his strong conviction that the complexity of human behavior can only be understood within the context of the "whole person." His emphasis upon the "holistic view of personality," namely, that the person reacts as an integrated organism and that his unity cannot be derived from mere behaviorism, is at the core of his therapy. It is the "self" which constitutes the focus of his analysis for it is the fundamental center of human personality. His theory of personality development is based upon this conviction. "The self, or self-concept," says Rogers, "is defined as an organized, consistent, conceptual gestalt composed of perceptions of the characteristics of the 'I' or 'me' to others and to various aspects of life, together with the values attached to these perceptions. It is a gestalt which is available to awareness though not necessarily in awareness." The "self-concept" is comprised of (1) what the individual thinks he is, (2) what he thinks he ought to be, and (3) and the "ideal self" or what he thinks he would like to be. This tripartite composition of the self constitutes the core of Rogers' personality theory.

Rogers does not belief that the "self" per se manages and monitors the individual's behavior but rather it "symbolizes" the individual's conscious experiences of the world — who he thinks he is, who he thinks he ought to be, and who he thinks he wants to be. He discounts, not possibly the reality of unconscious data, but its irrelevance to the individual's self-concept and its viability in the therapeutic situation for it is the individual's own self-understanding, as he explains it, describes it, characterizes it, that is important therapeutically. Phenomenology trumps unconscious data as the basis for psychological therapy, says Rogers for the structure of the self is formed through the individual's interaction with the familial, social, and cultural environment. The "content of one's self-concept," argued Rogers, is fundamentally a social product and not the result of the bombardment of the psyche with unconscious and repressed data.

Therefore, there are identifiable components needed for the development of a healthy self-concept and when they are absent or twisted from experience, the individual suffers. First, Rogers suggests that every person has a basic desire for warmth, respect, admiration, love, and acceptance from people important in his life. He calls this the "need for positive regard." Whether innate or social learned, this drive is strong from the earliest days of childhood. A person as infant, child, adolescent, or adult, he believes will do almost anything to meet this innate need for "positive regard." There is a reciprocal component to this drive as well, namely, in the giving of this positive regard, one receives it in turn. The reciprocity of positive regard is a strong re-enforcer of social relationships. The self, says Rogers, is profoundly influenced by this need and rather than suggest that individuals are driven to satisfy the demands and expectations of their "self-concept," he argues that people are driven to satisfy their need for positive regard, both to give it and to receive it.

Where there is a conflict between what the individual's wants in service to his "self" and what he recognizes as in service to his "need" for regard, Rogers call this "incongruence." "This, as we see it, is the basic estrangement in man. He has not been true to himself, to his own natural organism valuing of experience, but for the sake of preserving the positive regard of others has now come to falsify some of the values he experiences and to perceive them only in terms based upon their value to others." The conflict internally, that is, "incongruency," is the result of the individual choosing to service his need for positive regard at the expense of serving his own self's perceived personal needs. The conflict often leads to psychological stress, tension, and mental illness. "Yet," Rogers continues, "this has not been a conscious choice, but a natural — and tragic — development in infancy. The path of development toward psychological maturity is the undoing of this estrangement in man's functioning. The achievement of a self which is congruent with experience leads to the restoration of a unified organism valuing process as the regulator of behavior." Too often, it is the "people pleaser" who emerges from this incongruity, the individual who is so drive to please the other person that he forgets to please himself in the process.

Within the context of self-concept development within every individual from childhood is the presence of "conditional positive regard," namely, that situation in the family and society in which the individual is the recipient of positive regard only so long as that individual conforms to the expectations of the positive regard provider. In other words, positive regard is contingent upon compliance with outside expectations of family and society members. "I will love you so long as," or "only if" situations constitute conditional positive regard. This situation, Rogers believes, is detrimental to the child's ability to become a fully function-ing and self-actualized individual. The child, and eventually the adult, "relinquishes" ownership of his own needs and desires in order to conform to the "conditions" laid out by the parent, the family, and society for the giving of positive regard. The individual runs the serious risk of "losing himself" to himself in the process of conforming to the conditions established by others for the giving of positive regard. The "condition of worth" is compliance with the expectations of others, regardless of one's own sense of what is valued. This was painfully true in Rogers' own personal life as a child raised in an extremely restrictive religious home environment.

To counter act the mental health dangers of "conditional positive regard," Rogers developed the concept of "unconditional positive regard" and this concept characterizes all of his psychotherapeutic practice and theorizing about psychological treatment. In light of his own childhood experience, Rogers developed this concept as a counterpoise to the detrimental character of the conditions of worth operative in conditional positive regard. He believed strongly that it is possible to give and receive positive regard without attaching it to behavioral compliance. Positive regard can be given to individuals in situations where the behavior of the other individual is not necessarily to the liking of the positive regard giving individual. This requires every individual to be accepted and respected for who and what they are, without conditions of ifs, ands, or buts. Such unconditional positive regard is most evident in a mother's love of a misbehaving child. Parental love is not, then, given to the child when and only when the child "conforms" to the parents' behavioral expectations but love, positive regard, is given "unconditionally." Rogers was quick to criticize the Christian saying from Jesus, "You are my friends if you do what so ever I tell you." This is conditional worth and not love.

Rogers believes that children raised in the unconditional positive regard familial environment, "then no conditions of worth would develop, self-regard would be unconditional, the needs for positive regard and self-regard would never be at variance with organism evaluation, and the individual would continue to be psychologically adjusted, and would be fully functioning. This chain of events is hypothetically possible, and hence important theoretically, though it does not appear to occur in actuality." Discipline is not absent from the family environment, but the circumstances under which it is used and understood by both the child and the parent are radically different when disassociated from self-worth. The creation of an unconditional love "atmosphere" provides the mechanism for a positive use of discipline wherein the child can grow into a fully functioning and potentially self-actualized person with a deep and unchallenged sense of self worth.

Growing out of Rogers' understanding of the nature of the experience of "incongruity" were the experiences of "threat," "anxiety," and "defense." These three very common experiences are all interrelated and are manifested in the individual's awareness or lack of awareness of any incongruous situation. Every individual strives for what Rogers calls "consistency" in behavior, attempting at all times to keep an even keel in interpersonal relationships based upon the individual's self-concept. Where there is an incongruency between the individual's self-concept and the social situation making demands upon him inconsistent with his idea of himself, that individual feels a "threat." The threat in Rogers' theory occurs when a person recognizes an incongruity between his self-concept and its condition of worth corollary and the experience which precipitates the incongruity. This "threatening" situation is not always self-evidently conscious but the individual feels "anxious" by the encounter. Whenever this experience of incongruity exists in the individual's encounter where self-concept and outside experience are at odds, the individual feels a sense of vulnerability and often personality disorganization. Anxiety is, then, an emotional response to a threat to the individual's self-concept such that there is real danger of a debilitating discrepancy between the person and the situation.

When this situation arises, namely, a perceived conflict between self-concept and objective situation, the individual attempts to protect himself by the use of a defense mechanism. The process of defense, explains Rogers, is the behavioral response of the individual to the threat and the goal is for the reestablishment and maintenance of the self-concept. "This goal," Rogers continues, "is achieved by the perceptual distortion of the experience in awareness, in such a way as to reduce the incongruity between the experience and the structure of the self, or by the denial of any experience, thus denying any threat to the self." The production of defenses, then, is the individual's primary method of protecting himself, his self-concept, and his self-worth.

These defense mechanisms are of two kinds, says Rogers. There is the "perceptual distortion" and the "denial." The first occurs when an incongruent experience is allowed into an individual's perception but only in a form that makes it consistent with that individual's self-image and not something alien to his own experience. Thus, when an experience occurs challenging the individual but not outside the sphere of possibility, that individual employs a defense mechanism to explain the "distortion" in the experience rather than denying its reality. This occurs when someone is caught steeling in a situation in which that individual is conscious of the fact that even though he is not habitually a thief, it can, does, and might happens that he takes something that is really not his. This often occurs with employees of a company who help themselves to various items, aware that it is theft, but explaining to their own satisfaction that it is acceptable behavior. This, Rogers calls, "rationalization." Perceptual distortion produces rationalization thereby allowing an individual to maintain his self-concept without any or much jeopardy. However, in the case of "denial" as a defense mechanism, the individual attempts to protect their self-concept by simply denying that the situation of incongruity has occurred. When this defense mechanism, much more so than the previous one, is permitted to reign in a person's life, there is grave potential for the development of mental illness.

Throughout his writing career, Rogers made much of what he called the "good life" in which he used a term for that experience, namely, the "fully functioning person." the good life, for Rogers, is not a static state of experience, but a process, a direction, a way of living and comporting oneself through all of life's trials and tribulations. The good life "is a process of movement in a direction which the human organism selects when it is inwardly free to move in any direction. The general qualities of this selected direction appear to have a certain universality," Rogers contents, and "the person who is psychologically free moves in the direction of becoming a more fully functioning person." There are five major personality traits of such individuals and we will recite them briefly here. (1) Openness to experience (wherein the individual is not temperamentally closed to new situations, encounters, opportunities, challenges), (2) Existential living (wherein the individual is ready and willing to face what ever may come his way with hope, courage, and fortitude, (3) Organismic trusting (wherein the individual has confidence in his ability to make sound decisions and to act upon them with assurance of their wisdom, (4) Experiential freedom (wherein the individual embraces the possibilities of life without false or shallow constraints superimposed by family and society but with a willingness to explore possibilities for living), and (5) Creativity (wherein the individual is fully at liberty to venture into new realms of experiential living and expressiveness of life's possibilities. "The good life," Rogers expounds, "involves a wider range, a greater richness, than the constricted living in which most of us find ourselves. To be a part of this process means that one is involved in the frequently frightening and frequently satisfying experience of a more sensitive living, with greater range, greater variety, greater richness."

The juxtaposition of Rogerian psychology and that of Freud and Skinner is most profoundly realized in their differences over the nature of the human person. The Third Force of humanistic psychology was intentionally launched to counter the negativity and pessimism of both Freud's determinism and Skinner's behaviorism. Eight distinguishing traits are counterpoised in these schools of thought with Rogers and the phenomenological humanists on the one hand and the psychoanalysts and behaviorists on the other. First is that of freedom versus determinism, with Rogers strongly for the former and Freud and Skinner quite conspicuously on the side of the latter. Freedom, for Rogers, is an indispensable characteristic of human nature and without it the fully functioning individual has no chance of self-actualization. Again, rationality versus irrationality characterizes the radical distinction between these schools of thought. For Rogers, the human person is essentially a rational being, controlling and directing his own life when given the opportunity and, with help, can correct misdirection in one's life in a way that Freud and Skinner could never conceive nor would they allow. Holism, for Rogers, is the contra to behaviorism's "elementalism," by which is meant the behaviorist's happy dissecting of the human personality into elemental parts for analysis whereas with the humanists the person is treated and respected as an entity in its entirety.

A further distinction has to do with the difference between "constitutionalism" and "environmentalism," with the former on the side of the humanists who would have known that individuals are constituted of an innate tendency to self-actualization, whereas the behaviorists would have us rely upon the organic and instinctual situation of the individual as determinate in behavior. Whereas Skinner and Freud would emphasize the "objectivity" of the human person's behavioral modalities of being without reference to the individual's own self-understanding, Rogers would have us know that the human person is essentially a "subjective" being with thought process and behavioral modalities employed at his own initiative and to his own desired ends. Again, Rogers would have us know that the human person is "proactive" rather than "reactive" to life's situations and that the positive view of the human person is one in which every individual has the ability and is encouraged to assume responsibility for his actions rather than rely helplessly upon his instinctual urges and unconscious cuing for behavioral responses.

We are a proactive being rather than a mere reactive animal say the humanists of the Third Force. Because human beings are pontificated toward self-actualization, every individual is "heterostatic" rather than "homeostatic," that is to say, every person is in a mode of action, moving towards greater fulfillment, greater self-actualization, rather than bond and gagged by the instinctual and unconscious variables operative in his life but outside his control. Man is moving forward, not staked to his mere animal confines. And, finally, Roger would emphasize "knowability" whereas the behaviorists would claim "unknowability" as our life situation and destiny. Because of his embracing of the phenomenological school of psychology, Roger believed that man cannot use scientific knowledge to better understand who and what we are without a much greater reliance upon our own capacity at self-understanding. We are not merely the objective subject of scientific enquiry, but we are the subjective focus of interpersonal self-understanding. Science can help, but it must serve rather than dominate our enquiry.

Early on in our discussion, we called attention to the "evolution" of Rogerian psychotherapeutic methods of treatment, moving from a non-directive to client-centered to finally person-to-person center focus. In this context, Rogers has identified six conditions necessary for the therapeutic relationship to be beneficial. In closing, we will itemize these and comment briefly. (1) Two persons are in psychological contact (wherein two individuals, one self-defined as therapist and the other as client, meet together to address a personal issue of the client; (2) The client is in a state of incongruence, being vulnerable or anxious (wherein the situation presumes an interactive relationship of the two individuals addressing the incongruent feelings of the client), (3) The therapist is congruent or integrated in the relationship (by which is meant that this individual is aware of his role, his situation, and his responsibility in relationship to the client), (4) The therapist experiences unconditional positive regard for the client (such that the client does not raise defenses and is rather openly convergent with the therapist about his situation of anxiety), (5) The therapist experiences an empathic understanding of the client's internal frame of reference and endeavors to communicate this experience to the client (such that the client is enabled to better see and assess the situation which has arisen in his live which has produced the incongruence), and (6) The communication to the client of the therapist's empathic understanding and unconditional positive regard is to a minimal degree achieved (thereby setting the client on the road to recovering or discovering a sense of self-worth and fulfillment). Roger's person-to-person therapeutic method is a reflection of his whole image of man in general and more specifically of the therapist as a facilitator of personal growth and of the client towards self-actualization. Believing individuals are innately inclined to personal fulfillment, Rogers is ever optimistic about the healing process. His phenomenological theory has produced a great deal of research dealing with self-concept and his methodology has been widely adopted by various schools of psychotherapy, and not least with the ranks of pastoral counselors who have benefited the most and utilized his method extensively in their training and practice. Without question, Rogers and his followers have set a high standard of excellence in theory and practice.

Chapter VIII

Harry Stack Sullivan
and Interpersonal Psychoanalysis

BIOGRAPHICAL SKETCH

Herbert "Harry" Stack Sullivan was born on the 21st of February, 1892, in a small farming village called Norwick in New York State. The only surviving child of a poor Irish family, his childhood was lonely and uneventful, exacerbated by the fact that his family were the only Catholics in an all Protestant town. His father, Timothy Sullivan, was quiet and distant and his mother, Ella Stack Sullivan, with whom he was close, was sickly and of a complaining nature. Two sons died in infancy before Harry's birth and, needless to say, this bore heavily upon his mother. She was unhappy in marriage, having chosen a mate well below her family's station in life, as she thought of it romantically back in Ireland, and she was not disinclined to verbalize her disappointment in marriage and with life to her only son and companion. When Harry was three, his mother disappeared for about eighteen months, probably for a mental hospital stay, during which time he was cared for by his maternal grandmother whose Gaelic accent was often indecipherable to the child. When his grandmother died in 1903, a maiden aunt came to share the duties of motherhood so, in a sense, he had two mothers to raise him. As a child with only one friend, a little boy named Clarence Bellinger up the road who, interestingly enough, himself became a psychiatrist in adulthood, Harry invented several imaginary playmates but remained essentially an outsider during his school years. It is said that his Irish brogue was strong and his high marks set him apart from his peers at school. Brilliant and taciturn, "Harry" was an outstanding student and was groomed, not for farm work, but for university. He graduated, at the top of his high school class, earlier than most of his peers.

At sixteen, he was off to Cornell University to which he had won a scholarship from the State of New York, but, for various speculative reasons offered up by friends and relations in his home town, Harry did not graduate with a major in physics as he had planned but failed out his second semester. For two years, he disappeared and often referred to his hospitalization during this time for a mental breakdown. However, in 1911, he entered medical school and completed his studies in 1915 but did not receive his diploma until he was able to pay his outstanding tuition debt in 1917, He graduated without a sterling academic record from the Chicago College of Medicine and Surgery, a legitimate but somewhat disreputable institution not unlike many at the time in all large cities. He always spoke disparagingly of the quality of medical education he received and the school was the same year he received in diploma. Because of his poor training and virtually nothing in psychiatry, he was not exposed to the major theoretical systems in psychiatry and psychology of the day. This later proved to be an advantage in the development of his own school of thought.

During these trying years of effort to establish himself, he worked with schizophrenic patients at various hospitals, demonstrating a notable capacity to bring some success in dealing with schizophrenics using what he was already calling interpersonal therapy. This approach he was developing involved the training of staff to enact safe, corrective interpersonal interactions with the patients, arguing as he did that the institutional environment was artificial and counterproductive to personality development. He subse-quently served as a staff physician in the U.S. Army but two years later, during which time his fortunes were neither sterling nor well documented, he landed a position at the St. Elizabeth's Hospital in Washington, D.C, where, without any previous training in psychiatry what so ever, he was most fortunate in working with the notable Dr. William Alanson White, an early and successful psychiatrist trained in the Freudian school of psychoanalysis. Additionally, clinical research at Sheppard and Enoch Pratt Hospital consumed a portion of his life and passion from 1923 to 1930 as did a brief appointment in the University of Maryland's School of Medicine. He quickly established a reputation for success-fully treating patients with schizophrenia and began to write and publish his research findings.

During what he called his "Baltimore period" of theoretical development, he was engaged in extensive clinical experience and reach with schizophrenics. It was here that he began to think about interpersonal relations as a key ingredient in the therapeutic treatment of the mentally ill. In attempting to decipher the non-sensical speech of the schizophrenic, he realized that their illness was a means of coping with anxiety generated from a social or interpersonal environment rather than of biogenic origins. (After his death, DNA research has shown that Chromosome 11 is absent in 89% of the cases of schizophrenia.)

By 1931, he was sufficiently well-established and known to be asked to participate, indeed, even lead an initiative which led to the creation of the Washington School of Psychiatry. At this time he moved to New York where he developed a large and lucrative private psychotherapeutic practice and, interestingly enough, underwent 300 hours of pscyhoanalysis from Dr. Clara Thompson, a well established Freudian therapist. In later years, he was both a professor and head of the department of psychiatry at the Georgetown University Medical School and subsequently served as the president of the William Alanson White Psychiatric Foundation. Part of his role was to serve as editor of a newly created and soon to be considered internationally distinguished journal, *Psychiatry*, commenced in 1938, while simultaneously serving as chairman of the council of Fellows of the Washington

School of Psychiatry. During these very productive years, he became colleagues and friends of Edward Sapir, a cultural anthropologist, and Harold Lasswell, a political scientist, both from the University of Chicago. Of special relevance to his theory-building enterprise of international relations was his friendship with George Herbert Mean, Robert Ezra Park, and W. I. Thomas, all international distinguished sociologists at the University of Chicago. Other major figures with whom he came in contact and established personal friendships with include such professionally distinguished persons as Karen Horney, Erich Fromm, Frieda Fromm-Reichmann, and of special mention is Adolf Meyer. These experiences greatly broadened Sullivan's grasp of the behavioral and social sciences which eventually had a profound effect upon his theory of personality.

On the 14th of January, 1949, he died of a persistent cardiovascular disease while visiting Paris, having been attending an international conference, the World Federation for Mental Health which he helped found, in Amsterdam where his life's work was being discussed in some depth, both positively and negatively. He was buried in Arlington National Cemetery, having had a well-respected term of service in the U.S. Army as a practicing psychiatrist during and following the 2nd World War.

Sullivan never married though he did adopt a young man who was considered by all his friends as his "son," and, though considered anti-Catholic and non-religious by his friends and colleagues, his will called for a Catholic burial which he received. One distinguishing characteristic of his interpersonal psychotherapy was his desire, not always realized, to stay away from professional nomenclature when speaking of human relations. "I think," he wrote, "we should try to pick a word in common usage in talking about living and clarify just what we mean by that word, rather than to set about diligently creating new words by carpentry of Greek and Sanskrit roots." In spite of his desire and intent, his system itself produced a plethora of neologisms which requires a glossary to wade through them.

CLASSIC TEXT CONSIDERED

In 1939, the William Alanson White Foundation decided that a series of lectures should be given to honor the memory of White, a colleague of Sullivan's, who had died in 1937, and, of course, Sullivan was chosen to give the first series. He actually gave five lectures to small groups in an auditorium in a building owned by the Department of the Interior in Washington, DC. In these lectures, Sullivan made his first public attempt to present both a comprehensive and well-thought-out explanation of his concept of personality development including psychiatric disorders and treatment. In February of 1940, they were all published in the journal, *Psychiatry*, at the insistence of Sullivan's friends and colleagues, but against his best judgment. He was not pleased with his performance but finally consented and they appeared. Not surprisingly, they attracted much attention within the psychiatric and social science communities and in the following years many mental health and social science professional workers wrote to secure copies of this issue of the periodical. Finally, in 1947, much to the chagrin of Sullivan who believed his presentation of his thoughts was "grossly inadequate," a new printing of these lectures came out again in *Psychiatry*. This issue was in hardback and carried the somewhat dubious title of *Conceptions of Modern Psychiatry*. This was actually his own book, at least in his lifetime, to see the light of day though several subsequent volumes of his lectures and essays, all touted to be Sullivan's books, finally appeared. This one, however, sold 13,000 copies over the next several years and the William Alanson White Foundation gained considerable attention because of them. Under the same title, this book was published four years after the death of Sullivan and it still sells well each year. Sullivan, however, denounced many of the premature conceptual developments in the work and discounted its value.

Nevertheless, it is a pivotal work for our consider-ation and a few remarks are justified before we move to the driving concepts and theories of Sullivan's notions of personality. "Psychiatry," he wrote, "is the study of processes that involve or go on between people. The field of psychiatry is the field of interpersonal relations, under any and all circumstances in which these relations exist." This is the thesis set forth by Sullivan in this book. It is the first place where he expressed the central ides of his theory of personality. Through his development of the theory, he made not only a vital contribution in the treatment of mental disorder — in particular, schizophrenia — but he opened an entirely new approach to the study of human personality. In the view of many analyists, he made the most original contribution to psychiatry since Freud. Rollo May has gone on record as saying, "As Freud was the prophet for the Victorian age of sexual suppression, Sullivan is the prophet for our schizoid age — our age of unrelatedness, in which, beneath all the chatter of radio and newspapers and all the multitudes of 'contact,' people are often strangers to each other." His book, *Conceptions of Modern Psychiatry,* consists of reprints of the first William Alanson White Memorial Lectures, delivered by Sullivan in 1939, as we have said. They are profound and open a whole new world of interpretation of the nature of personality and the practice of psychiatry as an interpersonal relations science.

In this work, he created a new viewpoint which is known today as the "interpersonal theory of psychiatry." Sullivan's fundamental emphasis related to a theory of personality which is a "relatively enduring pattern of recurrent interpersonal situations which characterize a human life." Radically shifting from the psychoanalytic focus on the unconscious, Sullivan brought to his clinical research and practice a behavioral and social science perspective which had not been considered a significant component of personality theory until now. He argued that the concept of "personality" is itself a hypothetical entity which cannot be isolated from interpersonal situations and, indeed, interpersonal behavior is all that is observable about personality. The rest, he suggests, is strictly metaphorical speculation and creative imagery. It is futile and fruitless to speak of a person's personality outside the social interactive matrix of the living person. Not discounting the significance of heredity and the maturation process as affected by the physical environment, the real thing that determines the nature of a human person is the social interaction of that person with others.

Never before had such an attempt been made to merge psychiatry and social psychology. His theory of personality is the product of such a merger and it is greatly enriched by his acquaintance with and utilization of the social sciences. He writes: "The general science of psychiatry seems to me to cover much the same field as that which is studied by social psychology, because scientific psychiatry has to be defined as the study of interpersonal relations, and this in the end calls for the use of the kind of conceptual framework that we now call *field theory*. From such a standpoint, personality is taken to be hypothetical. That which can be studied is the pattern of processes which characterize the interaction of personalities in particular recurrent situations or fields which include the observer." This attitude about the place and relevance of the "observer" in the clinical situation became a benchmark of Sullivan's innovative approach to the therapeutic encounter. He was, of course, influenced by the science philosopher, Heisenberg, on this point particularly.

Modern psychiatry as defined and practiced by Sullivan consists of a study of personality characteristics which can be directly observed in the context of interpersonal relationships. Systems of psychiatry based on statements about what is going on in the patient's mind are therefore similar to a system of thought which is built on axioms such as "All events are controlled by Divine Providence." The truth or falseness of this statemetn cannot be established by things that reasonably well educated people can see, hear, and feel. Much human experience can be cited to support such a statement, and much human experience can be cited to nullify it, but it is so set up that it must always remain a matter of faith. For Sullivan, a "personality characteristic" is defined as the things which people can see, hear, and feel in their relationships with other individuals. This is the most fundamental working hypothesis in his personality theory.

Though Sullivan is only willing to allow personality to be purely hypothetical apart from the actually observable reality of social interaction, he does assert that it is a dynamic center of various processes which occur in a series of interpersonal fields. This "dynamism" is a key concept in his overall personality theory. He gives significant place to these processes by identifying and naming them as he constructs a platform of their characteristics. These processes, then, are *dynamisms, personifications*, the *self-system*, and *cognitive processes*. Let's explore each briefly here as they constitute the backbone of his major work, *Conceptions of Modern Psychiatry*.

The smallest unit of study in interpersonal relation-ships is what he calls "dynamism." It constituted an energy transference which meant any unit of behavior, either actual act or mental experience. They become habitual ways of acting which involve the physical body of the person, such as the mouth, hands, arms, legs, etc. These dynamisms can then be broken down into a plethora of subsets, such as the fear dynamism, intimate dynamism, etc. The dynamisms which are distinctively human in character are those which characterize one's interpersonal relations and function primarily to satisfy some basic needs of the individual. Three major dynamisms are malevolence, lust, and intimacy. Malevolence is the driving dynamism that one is living among one's own personal enemies and, if this negative dynamism emerges early in a child's life, he may find it difficult ever in adulthood to reach a fully trusting relationship with another person. Sullivan expressed it poignantly: "Once upon a time everything was love, but that was before I had to deal with people." Lust is another driving dynamism of the individual. Lust for Sullivan consists of the complex urges, feelings, and interpersonal actions which have genital sexual activity as their distant or immediate goal; lust begins in early adolescence. Sullivan rejected the Freudian concept of sexuality and suggested that it was more or less inconsequential in childhood and early adolescence, but lust constitutes a major driving force in later adolescence. Intimacy for Sullivan is a profoundly positive dynamism potentially. It occurs when the well-being of another person is as important to an individual as his own sell-being. It does not occur in parent-child relationships and does not involve lust or sexual behavior and, says he, occurs only between members of the same sex. Lust becomes, then, a contaminant of intimacy for lust seeks to serve itself rather than the other person.

Personifications consist of an image that an individual has of himself or of some other person. It is a complex of feelings, attitudes, and conceptions that grows out of experience with need-satisfaction and anxiety and, for example, Sullivan speaks often of the "good-mother," "bad-mother," and "overprotective mother" as examples. When these personifications are shared by a large social grouping, they become stereotypes such as "all Irishman are drunks," "all Catholics lie," etc., and these stereotypes are held by social groups without experience of their reality but of a shared personification of imagined peoples' behavior.

The self-system is another dynamism which is crucial to personality structure. It functions as a security measure to protect the individual from anxiety. In order to avoid or minimize actual or potential anxiety, the person adopts various types of protective measures and supervisory controls over his behavior. These security measures form the self-system which sanctions certain forms of behavior, such as the "good-me" self, and forbids other forms of behavior, such as the "bad-me" self.

Sullivan's unique contribution to the role of cognition in personality theory has to do with his development of a threefold classification of experiences, for, says he, experiences occur in three different modes — *protaxic, parataxic, and syntaxic.* These experiential modes merit a brief description of each in order to appreciate their relevance to Sullivan's interpersonal relations description of psychiatry. Sometimes called "types of experience" and sometimes called "types of cognition," this tripartite foundation of personality encounters are worthy of close attention.

The simplest and most fundamental mode of experiencing reality at the beginning of life is what Sullivan chose to call the *prototoxic* mode. It consists of essentially a flowing of sensations, feelings, and images without any necessary connection between them, a kind of "stream of consciousness," if you will. Sullivan himself describe it this way: "It may be regarded as the discrete series of momentary states of the sensitive organism." It occurs, of course, during the earliest months of infancy and must precede the others as a preparation for them. The *parataxic* mode of thinking, Sullivan explains, consists of seeing causal relationships between events that occur at about the same time but which are not logically related. Getting the connection wrong is what this mode of experience is all about. It is magical thinking, says he, for there is no logical connection between two events experienced by the child in which the child assumes there is. It is essentially the "elementary externalization of causality." In childhood it occurs regularly when the child assumes that something he has done is the cause of something that is quite decidedly unrelated but he thinks it is. In adulthood, the residuals of parataxis modes of experiencing occur in such things as the presumed relationship between "praying hard" and "getting well."

Finally, the third and most advanced mode of experience is called *syntaxic* and it corresponds to logical, analytical thought. Syntaxic experience of reality thus presupposes the ability to understand physical and spatial causality, and the ability to predict causes from knowledge of their effects. The meaning of words and the use of numbers constitutes the most poignant examples of the function of syntaxic experience and when the child learns the meaning of specific words and their uses and the nature of numbers and how they work, the child has reached this level of experiential sophistication needed in the development of interpersonal relationships.

CONCEPTS AND THEORIES

Harry Stack Sullivan's distinguishing contribution to contemporary psychiatry was his heavy emphasis upon the social factors which contribute to the development of human personality. Though schooled in Freudian psychoanalysis, he was not a Freudian in the sense that he differed from Freud in viewing the significance of the early parent-child relationship as being an early quest for security rather than, as in Freudian psychoanalysis, primarily sexual in origin and nature.

Drawing from his own personal life's story, Sullivan saw this child-mother relationship as central, not the sexual drive of libidinal instincts. Sullivan, on the other hand, was intent upon integrating the multiple disciplines of the behavioral and social sciences into the work of psychiatry such that sociology and social psychology in the tradition of George Herbert Mead and Charles Horton Cooley proved most helpful in Sullivan's eventual development of what became known as interpersonal psychiatry, later interpersonal psychotherapy. He was not averse to reaching across disciplinary lines for theory and method, from evolution to communications, from learning theory to social organization. It was "interpersonal relations" which, he believed, constituted the fundamental ingredient in the personality structure.

Sullivan was adverse to that form of psychiatry and clinical psychotherapy which dealt with mental illness through the study of institutionally-isolated patients. He had extensive experience in working with the mentally ill, particularly with schizophrenics, and he felt the institutionally committed constituted a weak source of clinical insight. Personality characteristics, for instance, he felt were determined by the interpersonal relationships between therapists and patients and that the institutional environment was artificial and counterproductive. Sullivan contended that personality develops according to people's perception of how others view them. "Others," in Sullivan thought, included personifications, like the government, as well as imaginary and idealized figures like Jesus or Moses or even movie stars. He believed, based upon his own clinical encounters with severely mentally ill patients, that cultural forces were largely responsible for their psychological condition. He contended that a healthy personality is the result of healthy relationships and that most of what goes in our society as mental illness is not "biogenic," but rather "sociogenic." Sullivan refused to employ the concept of "personality" as a unique, individual, and unchanging entity as so often was the case with traditionalists. He much preferred to define personality as a manifestation of the interaction between individuals, namely, interpersonal relations.

Sullivan's clinical work in a variety of settings through several years of medical assignments led him to firmly believe in the impact interpersonal relationships have upon personality development. He noted that individuals tend to carry distorted views and unrealistic expectations of others into their relationships. His solution was to become, as a clinical psychotherapist, a "participant observer" in dealing with his clients, taking a more active therapeutic stance than the traditional psychoanalytic "blank screen" approach popular at the time and particularly with the Freudian school of psychoanalysis. By focusing upon what he called "interpersonal behavior," he would observe the client's reaction to the therapist and the therapeutic environment. He believed that emotional well-being could be achieved by making an individual "aware" of their dysfunctional interpersonal patterns of interaction and thereby grow into a healthy self-awareness of their interactive behavior.

Before we consider Sullivan's now paradigmatic stages of personality development, we should say something about his concept of human nature and, it has been suggested by him many times, it can be summed up in the expression, "everyone is much more simply human than otherwise." Having made this his standard operational modality, he utilized it throughout his career and summed up its meaning this way: In other words, the differences between any two instances of human personality from the lowest grade imbecile to the highest-grade genius — are much less striking than the difference between the least-gifted human being and a member of the nearest other biological genus." Sullivan was outspoken on this point.

Denying that there were any really operative instincts left in the human person, and thus separating himself profoundly from Freud and the classical school of psychoanalysis, Sullivan contended that it is the social environment in which we mature that determines the effectiveness of our maturation. Interpersonal relationships are the essence of human development. We are only human in so far as we develop within the context of other people. We need to learn to compete, cooperate, and compromise with other children as we mature in order to maintain mental health. "Personal individuality is an illusion." We exist only in relationship with other people. When we mature within a healthy social environment, this positive progression of interpersonal events leads to an integrated personality, an adult who is capable of establishing satisfying interpersonal relations and who is able to both give and receive love. This is the essence of the human personality.

Sullivan's ellaborate and well-developed description of the stages of human development were reminiscent of Freud's elaborate system. But, whereas Freud built his developmental scheme around the central core of childhood sexuality, Sullivan built his around the fundamental core of interpersonal relationships. There are seven developmental stages in his schema and we will just mention them briefly here before concluding with remarks about his therapeutic method. Infancy is from the beginning to about eighteen months, and the first expressions of the "self system" appear when the infant encounters and relates to the "good me", "bad me" feeding experience in relationship to his mother. Childhood commences with the acquisition of language and goes through the preschool years.

Syntaxic experience, Sullivan explained, develops and the child encounters and deals with the reality and necessity of living with others as peers and authority figures. The juvenile person corresponds to the grade school years to about age eleven and here interpersonal relations includes competition, cooperation, and comprise as developmental necessities. Preadolescence is short, eleven to thirteen more or less, and here intimacy emerges in relationship to same-sex peers and chums and marks the first real instance of what Sullivan calls "genuine human relations." Early adolescence commences the heterosexual years of stress and physical development and the intimacy dynamic is matched with lust and lasts through the beginning of the high school years when late adolescence produces the profound demands of complex interpersonal relationships and particularly heterosexual ones fraught with anxiety. Adulthood is arrived at with the composite of strengths and weaknesses in the personality which have developed through the interpersonal experiences of the maturing process.

Sullivan's psychotherapeutic methodology was quite unique to his own understanding of the function and nature of interpersonal relationships. Sullivan firmly believed, based upon his extensive clinical experience, that mental disorders derive from interpersonal failures and, therefore, therapeutic procedures must be based upon a genuine effort to improve the patient's relationship skills in dealing with others. In keeping with his overall worldview, interpersonal relation-ships constitute the core of psychotherapeutic treatment. In this situation, it is imperative that the therapist understand that his role is primarily that of a "participant observer," for, despite all protestations to the contrary from traditionalists, the therapist becomes necessarily part of an interpersonal, face-to-face relationship with the patient. This process actually creates the opportunity for the patient to establish a syntaxic communication with another person, namely, the therapist himself.

Because of the emphasis upon the therapeutic role being that of an "observer," the therapist is exempt from becoming "involved" with the patient but, as with the Freudian tradition, the therapist must establish a relationship based upon his role as an expert in relationships, not just a friend, chum, or colleague. Unlike the work of Carl Rogers, Sullivan is insistent that the therapist "not" become a friend of the patient, thereby destroying the "observational" character of the therapist's relationship to the patient. Sullivan had three primary objectives in the therapeutic situation. First, he intends to help the patient improve foresight, discover difficulties in interpersonal relations, and restore the ability to participate in consensually validated experiences. This occurs when three questions are addressed: (1) How can I best put into words what I wish to say to the patient?, (2) What is the general pattern of communication between us", and (3) What precisely is the patient saying to me? Simplistic? Certainly not!

The therapeutic interview is divided into four stages: (1) formal inception, (2) reconnaissance, (3) detailed inquiry, and (4) termination. Let's explicate just briefly the character of each stage. At the first meeting, the psychiatrist promotes confidence in the patient by demonstrating interpersonal skills and permits the patient to express the reasons for seeking therapy in the first place. The therapist, then, formulates tentative hypotheses regarding the declared cause for seeking treatment, and then decides on a possible course of action.

During reconnaissance, there is a general personal and social history established of the patient and the therapist in an attempt to determine how the patient came to develop a particular personality type. Here, the therapist asks specific questions about the patient's age, birth order, mother, father, education, occupational history, marriage, children, etc. Open ended questions are asked to invite the patient to feel free to express his emotional state at the time. Then, the detailed inquiry attempts to improve upon his understanding of the patient and the patient's understanding of his own situation, particularly articulating why he has sought therapy. The fourth and final stage of the interview is termination, or, in some cases, interruption. Of course, this means that the interview has come to an end. Quite commonly, the therapist gives the client "homework," something to do or some memory to recall for the next session. After each such session, the therapist makes copious notes about the session, what progress has been made and what issues have arisen that need addressing in the next session. For Sullivan, the therapeutic ingredient in this process is the face-to-face relationship between psychiatrist and patient, which permit's the patient to reduce anxiety and to communicate with others on the syntaxic level.

In some circles, Harry Stack Sullivan is considered the "father of modern psychiatry," but, of course, this is prior to the emergence of the psychiatrist as "meds monitor"! Today, unlike his day, psychiatry has been disastrously reduced to monitoring medication without the slightest effort or benefit of therapeutic counseling which has, by and large, been left to either the social worker or the pastoral counselor. Psychiatry can no longer function as the therapeutic dispenser it was from Freud to Sullivan because the insurance companies and the HMOs have precluded the affordability of such functions. Psychiatrist must dispense and monitor the psychopharmacological industry's involvement with clients and patients, leaving what counseling even occurs to a lower level of professionalism, namely, social workers and pastoral counselors. Of course, it is the patient and client who suffer, but such is the fee-driven market system operative in American society today.

CONCLUSION

From Freud to Sullivan is not only a monumental leap in time but a quantitative leap in personality theory and psychotherapeutic theories of practice. From the birth of Freud in 1856 to the death of Sullivan in 1949, the world of psychology and the practice of both psychiatry and psychotherapy have undergone a development comparable to that in biology and physics in the last hundred years. From Freud's fascination with the possibilities of exploring the "unconscious" of a patient through the use of dream interpretation, word associations, and hypnosis to Sullivan's clinically demonstrated insight into the fundamental nature of interpersonal relationships skills as the determiner of mental health, one can argue that the discipline of psychology has remade itself. From deterministic behaviorism to the Third Force is no easy leap and with the initial and somewhat overpowering influence of the "depth" psychologists, Freud and Jung, the gradual emergence of the humanistic school of psychotherapy under the leadership of such clinical practitioners as Maslow, Frankl, and Rogers is nothing short of profound.

Interpersonal psychotherapy arrived upon the scene just when it seemed that "depth" psychology of the psychoanalytic type was waning in terms of both interest in and viability for those in counseling, particularly those in pastoral counseling. The arrival of "the will to meaning" followed by the Third Force movement has reinvigorated counseling psychology like no previous theoretical development in the history of the field. With Franklian psychology more and more taking the field with power and influence, Rogerian client-centered therapy and Sullivan's interpersonal psychotherapy have likewise shared in this resurgence of professional interest in counseling psychology and pastoral counseling.

It is my hope that this journey through the lives and literature of the great thinkers over the past one hundreds years has brought a sense of historical continuity and a genuine sense of existential validation to the practice of counseling psychology and pastoral counseling. Whether logotherapy or interpersonal psychotherapy becomes the counseling modality one uses, it is helpful to know the connections of these various modes of clinical practice and their viability in the day-to-day counseling situation that professional psychologists and pastoral counselors encounter. If this book serves the needs of these professionals, I am pleased. What now needs to happen is for a similar study to be made of the post-Rogerian psychotherapeutic schools of thought but that I will happily leave to a younger and more currently connected author.

GLOSSARY OF TERMS

Terms are listed here as used in all schools of psychotherapy considered in this study. Special thanks to Jess Feist and Ann Graber for terms which proved most helpful in this collection.

Accusation Used by Adlerians as a safeguarding tendency whereby one protects magnified feelings of self-esteem by blaming others for one's own failures.

Activity The degree of activity is the level of energy or interest with which one moves toward finding solutions to life's problems as used in Adlerian psychology.

Actualizing tendency A Rogerian term referring to the tendency within all people to move toward completion or fulfillment of potentials.

Aesthetic needs A term used by Maslow which refers to human needs for art, music, beauty, etc. though they may be related to the basic conntative needs; aesthetic needs are a separate dimension.

Aggression An Adlereian term referring to safeguarding tendencies that may include depreciation or accusation of others, as well as self-accusation, all designed to protect exaggerated feelings of personal superiority by striking out against other people.

Aggression A Freudian term referring to one or two primary instincts or drives that motivate people. Aggression is the outward manifestation of the death instinct and is at least a partial explanation for wars, personal hostility, sadism, masochism, and murder.

Analytical Psychology Theory of personality and approach to psychotherapy founded by Carl Jung.

Anima Jungian archetype that represents the feminine side in the personality of males and originates from men's inherited experiences with women.

Animus   Jungian archetype that represents the masculine component in the personality of females and originates from women's inherited experiences with men.

Anticathexis   A Freudian term referring to a check or restraint upon an instinctual drive.

Anxiety   A felt, affective, unpleasant state accompanied by physical sensation.

Apathy A term used by Sullivan to refer to the dynamism that reduces tensions of needs through the adoption of an indifferent attitude.

Archetypes   Jung's concept that refers to the content of the collective unconscious.

Attitude   Jung's specialized usage referring to a predisposition to act or react in a characteristic manner, that is, in either an introverted or an extraverted direction.

Autistic language   A term used by Sullivan to refer to private or parataxic language, which makes little or no sense to other people.

Autoeroticism   Self-gratification and in Freudian terms, infants are seen as exclusively autoerotic since their interest in pleasure is limited to themselves.

Aversive stimulus A painful or undesired stimulus which, when associated with a response, decreases the tendency of that response to be repeated in similar situations.

B-love A concept developed by Maslow to refer to love between self-actualizing people characterized by the love for the "being of the other."

B-values   A concept developed by Maslow that refers to the values of self-actualizing people, including beauty, truth, goodness, justice, wholeness, etc.

Basic anxiety   A term from Maslow suggesting that anxiety arises from the inability to satisfy physiological and safety needs.

Behaviorism A school of psychology that limits its subject matter to observable behavior. John B. Watson is usually credited with being the founder of behaviorism, with b. F. Skinner its most notable proponent.

Castration complex   Freudian suggesting a condition that accompanies the Oedipus complex, but takes different forms in the two sexes. In boys it takes the form of castration anxiety, or fear of having one's penis removed, and it is responsible for shattering the Oedipus complex. In girls it takes the form of penis envy, or the desire to have a penis, and precedes and instigates the Oedipus complex.

Cathexis A Freudian term referring to a driving or urging force.

Client-centered therapy Approach to psychotherapy originated by Carl Rogers, which is based on respect for the person's capacity to grow within a nurturing climate.

Cognitive needs A Maslovian term suggesting needs for knowledge and understanding; related to basic or conative needs, yet operate on a different dimension.

Collective unconscious Jung's idea of an inherited unconscious. He believed that many of our acts are motivated by unconscious ideas that are beyond our personal experiences and originate with repeated experiences of our ancestors.

Complex A Jungian term suggesting an emotionally toned conglomeration of ideas, which comprise the contents of the personal unconscious. Jung originally used the Word Association Test to uncover complexes.

Compulsion neurosis Neurotic reaction characterized by phobias, obsessions, and compulsions.

Conditions of worth A term employed by Rogers to suggest restrictions or qualifications attached to one person's regard for another.

Congruence Rogers' term for the matching of organismic experiences with awareness, and with the ability to express those experiences. One of three "necessary and sufficient" therapeutic conditions.

Conscience As used by Freud, that part of the superego which results from experience with punishment and which, therefore, tells a person what is wrong or improper conduct. As used by Frankl, conscience "is that capacity which empowers a person to seize the meaning of a situation in its very uniqueness."

Conscious As used by Freud, a term referring to those mental elements in awareness at any given time.

Consensual validation   The agreement of two or more people on the meaning of experiences, especially language. In Sullivan's thought, consensually validated experiences are said to operate on the syntaxic level of cognition.

Constructing obstacles   Adler developed this term to suggest the safeguarding tendency characterized by a person creating a barrier to success so that self-esteem can be protected by either using the barrier as an excuse or by overcoming it.

Conversion hysteria   Neurotic reaction characterized by the transformation of repressed psychological conflicts into overt physical symptoms.

Counter transference   A Freudian concept referring to the strong undeserved feelings the therapist develops toward the patient during the course of treatment.   These feelings can be either positive or negative and are considered by most writers to be a hindrance to successful psychotherapy.

D-love   A term developed by Maslow to refer to deficiency love or affection (attachment) based on the lover's specific deficiency and the loved one's ability to satisfy that deficit.

Death instinct   A Freud concept which suggests one of two primary drives or impulses, the death instinct is also known as Thanatos or agression.

Deductive method   Approach to factor analytical theories of personality that gathers data on the basis of previously determined hypotheses or theory.   Reasoning from the general to the particular.

Defense mechanisms   A Freud concept referring to techniques such as repression, reaction formation, sublimation, etc., whereby the ego defends itself against the pain of anxiety.

Defensiveness   Rogers's term for the protection of the self-concept against anxiety and threat by denial and distortion of experiences inconsistent with it.

Denial   Roger's term for the blocking of an experience or some aspect of an experience from awareness because it is inconsistent with the self-concept.

Depreciation Adlerian safeguarding tendency whereby another's achievements are undervalued and one's own are overvalued.

Dereflection According to Frankl, dereflection focuses attention away from the situation. "…on two essential qualities of human existence, namely, man's capacities of self-transcendence and self-detachment."

Desacralization Maslow suggests that this is the process of removing respect, joy, awe, rapture, etc., from an experience resulting in the purification or objectifying of that experience.

Dissociation A term used by Sullivan to suggest the process of separating unwanted impulses, desires, and needs from the self-system.

Dynamisms Sullivan's terms for the relatively consistent patterns of action which characterize the person throughout a lifetime. Similar to traits or habit patterns.

Ecclesiogenic damage According to Frankl, damage caused by the clergy.

Ego A term used extensively by Freud and Freudians to refer to the province of the mind that refers to the "I" or those experiences which are owned (not necessarily consciously) by the person. As the only region of the mind in contact with the real world, the ego is said to serve the reality principle.

Ego A term used extensively by Jung and the Jungians to refer to the center of consciousness. In Jungian psychology the ego is of lesser importance than the more inclusive self and is limited to consciousness.

Ego-ideal In Freud terms, that part of the superego which results from experiences with reward and which, therefore, teach a person what is right or proper conduct.

Eidetic personifications Sullivan's concept for imaginary traits attributed to real or imaginary people in order to protect one's self-esteem.

Empathy Roger's term for the accurate sensing of the feelings of another and the communication of these perceptions. One of three "necessary and sufficient" therapeutic conditions.

Empathy Sullivan's term for an indefinite process through which anxiety is transferred from one person to another, for example from mother to infant.

Empirical   Based on experience, systematic observation, and experiment rather than logical reasoning or philosophical speculation.

Energy transformations   Sullivan's term for the overt or covert actions designed to satisfy needs or reduce anxiety.

Enhancement needs   Roger's term for the need to develop, to grow, and to achieve.

Erogenous zones Organs of the body that are especially sensitive to the reception of pleasure. In Freudian theory, the three principal erogenous zones are the mouth, anus, and genitals.

Excuses Adlerian safeguarding tendencies whereby the person, through the use of reasonable sounding justifications, becomes convinced of the reality of self-erected obstacles.

Existential   As used by Frankl, "…may be used in three ways: to (a) existence itself, I.e., the specifically human mode of being; (b) the meaning of existence; and © the striving to find a concrete meaning in personal existence, that is to say, the will to meaning."

Existential Analysis   As used by Frankl, psychotherapy whose starting-point and whose particular concern is making man conscious of his responsibility. It is the "analysis of the responsibility aspects of being human."

Existential frustration   In Frank's terms, a "frustration of the will-to-meaning which may lead to neurosis. … It is in itself neither pathological nor pathogenic. A man's concern, even his despair, over the worthwhile ness of life is a spiritual distress but by no means a mental disease."

Existential vacuum   A general sense of meaninglessness sand emptiness, an "inner void," an "abyss-experience" according to Frankl and Logotherapists, and it manifest itself "mainly in a state of boredom."

External evaluation   A Rogerian term for the conditions of worth placed on a person, which may then serve as a criterion for evaluating one's own conduct. Conditions of worth block growth and interfere with one's becoming fully functioning.

Extraversion A Jungian concept which refers to an attitude or type characterized by the turning outward of psychic energy so that the person is oriented toward the objective.

Feeling A Jungian concept which refers to a rational function that tells us the value of something. The feeling function can be either extraverted (directed toward the objective world) or introverted (directed toward the subjective world).

Fiction An Adlerian term used to refer to a belief or expectation of the future, which serves to motivate present behavior. The truthfulness of a fictional idea is immaterial since the person acts as if the idea were true.

Fixation A defense mechanism that arises when psychic energy is blocked at one stage of development, thus making change or psychological growth difficult.

Formative tendency A term used by Rogers to refer to the tendency in all matter to evolve from simpler to more complex forms.

Genital stage A period of life recognized in Freudian psychology beginning with puberty and continuing through adulthood. This second sexual stage of the person's life should not be confused with the phallic phase, which takes place during the first sexual stage, that is, during infancy.

Hesitating A terms used by Alderian psychologists applied to the safeguarding tendency characterized by vacillation or procrastination designed to provide a person with the excuse, "It's too late now."

Heuristic Pertaining to a method or theory that leads to the discovery of new information.

Hierarchy of needs A major concept in the work of Maslow which refers to the realization that needs are ordered in such a manner that those on a lower level must be satisfied before higher level needs become activated.

Holistic-dynamic Maslow's theory of personality, which streses both the unity of the organism and the motivational aspects of personality.

Humanistic psychology   Ill-defined term referring to those theories and systems of psychology which, in general, emphasize the power of the individual to make conscious rational decisions and which stress the primacy of humans to other beings.

Hyperintention In Franklian psychology, attempts to escape the existential vacuum by focusing on the pursuit of pleasure. The direct attention on pleasure defeats itself. "The more an individual aims at pleasure, the more he misses the aim."

Hysteria A Freudian term used to refer to a mental disorder characterized by conversion of repressed psychical elements into somatic symptoms such as impotency, paralysis, or blindness, where no physiological bases for these symptoms exist.

Id A key term in Freudian psychoanalytic theory which refers to that region of personality which is alien to the ego in that it includes experiences that have never been owned by the person. The id is the home base for all the instincts and its sole function is to seek pleasure, regardless of consequences.

Ideal self   A Rogerian terms used for one's view of self as one would like to be.

Idealization   An Adlerian safeguarding tendency whereby the individual, in order to maintain exaggerated feelings of inferiority, sets up an ideal model so that any real person, by comparison, will inevitably fall short and thus be depreciated.

Incongruence   A term used by Rogers to suggest the perception of discrepancies between organism self, self-concept, and ideal self.

Individual Psychology   Theory of personality and approach to psychotherapy founded by Alfred Adler.

Individuation Jung's term for the process of becoming a whole perso, that is, an individual with a high level of psychic development. Similar to Maslow's concept of self-actualization.

Inductive method   Approach to factor analytic theories of personality that gathers data with no preconceived hypotheses or theory in mind. Reasoning from the particular to the general.

Infantile state Freud's term for the first four or five years of life characterized by autoerotic or pleasure-seeking behavior and consisting of the oral, anal, and phallic substages.

Inferiority complex A term used by Adler to suggest the exaggerated or abnormally strong feelings of inferiority, which usually interfere with socially useful solutions to life's problems.

Instinct From the German "trieb" meaning drive or impulse, Freud used this term to refer to an internal stimulus that impels action or thought. The two primary instincts are sex and aggression.

Instinctoid needs Maslow developed this term to mean the needs that are innately determined, but can be modified through learning. The frustration of instinctoid needs leads to pathology. The use of the word "instinctual" would have served his system better as there was always confusion regarding this term.

Intimacy Sullivan used this term to refer to the conjunctive dynamism characterized by a close personal relationship with another person who is more or less of equal status.

Introversion Jung used this term to apply to an attitude or type characterized by the turning inward of psychic energy with an orientation toward the subjective.

Intuition Jung used this term to apply to an irrational function that involves perception of elementary data that are beyond our awareness. Intuitive people "Know" something without understanding how they know.

Irrational functions Methods of dealing with the world without evaluation or thinking. Sensing and intuiting are the two irrational functions.

Isolation A Freudian term used to characterize a defense mechanism; also a type of repression, whereby the ego attempts to isolate an experience by establishing a period of black-out affect immediately following that experience.

Latent dream content A term used by Freud for the underlying, unconscious meaning of a dream. Freud held that the latent content, which can only be revealed through dream interpretation, was more important than the surface, or manifest, dream content.

Libido Freud used this term to refer to the psychic energy of the life instinct; sexual drive or energy.

Life instinct Freud used this term for one or two primary drives or impulses, the life instinct is also called Eros or sex.

Logotherapy According to Frankl, "focuses on the meaning of human existence as well as on man's search for such a meaning. ... the striving to find a meaning in one's life is the primary motivational force in man. ... It is a psychotherapy which not only recognizes man's spirit, but actually starts from it."

Lust A term used by Sullivan for the isolating dynamism characterized by impersonal sexual interest in another.

Maintenance needs A Rogerian term for those basic needs which protect the status quo. They may be either physiological (e.g., food), or interpersonal (e.g., the need to maintain the current self-concept).

Malevolence Sullivan's term for those destructive behavior patterns characterized by the attitude that people are evil and harmful and that the world is a bad place to live.

Manadala A symbol, says Jung, that represents the striving for unity and completion. It is often seen as a circle within a square or a square within a circle.

Manifest dream content A central Freudian concept referring to the surface or conscious meaning of a dream. The manifest content of a dream is the story the dreamer can describe to others. Freud believed that the manifest level of a dream has no deep psychological significance and that the unconscious or latent level holds the key to the dream's true meaning.

Masculine protest Adler's term for the neurotic and erroneous belief held by some men and women that males are superior to females.

Maturity Freud used this term to mean the final psychosexual state following infancy, latency, and the genital period. Maturity would be characterized by a strong ego in control of the id and superego and by an ever-expanding realm of consciousness.

Though we all strive for maturity, Freud believed that only a very few individuals ever reach it.

Metamotivation   Maslow's terms for the motives of self-actualizing people including especially the B-values.

Metapathology   Maslow's terms for the illness characterized by absence of values, lack of fulfillment, and loss of meaning of life and resulting from deprivation of self-actualization needs.

Moving backward   Adler used this term to apply to the safeguarding of inflated feelings of of superiority by reverting to a more secure period of life.

Neurasthenia   Neurotic condition characterized by excessive fatigue, chronic aches and pains, and low motivational level.

Neurosis   A term signifying mild personality disorders, as opposed to the more severe psychotic reactions. Neuroses are generally characterized by one or more of the following: anxiety, hysteria, phobias, obsessive-compulsive reactions, depressing, chronic fatigue, and hypochondriacal reactions.

Noetic dimension The dimension of the human spirit containing our healthy core, where can be found such uniquely human attributes as will to meaning, ideas and ideals, creativity, etc.

Noogenic   A logo therapeutic term which refers to anything having to do with the "spiritual" core of one's personality. The word spiritual does not mean religious but rather it refers to the specifically human dimension of being human. Noetic phenomena is a dimension above the somatic and psychic.

Oedipus complex   The classic concept in Freudian psychoanalysis used to indicate the situation where the child of either sex develops feelings of love and/or hostility for the parent. In the smiple male Oedipus complex, the boy has incestuous feelings of love for the mother and hostility toward the father. The simple female Oedipus complex exists when the girl feels hostility for the mother and sexual love for the father.

Operational definition   A definition of a concept in terms of specific operations to be carried out by the observer.

Oral phase   Freud used this term to refer to the earliest phase of the infantile period. This stage is characterized by attempts to gain pleasure through the activity of the mouth, especially sucking, eating, and biting; corresponds roughly to the first 12 - 18 months of life.

Organ dialect   Adlerian term referring to the expression of a person's underlying intentions or style of life through a diseased or dysfunction bodily organ.

Organismic self   Roger used this concept as a more general term than self-concept, the organismic self includes the entire person, including those aspects of existence beyond awareness.

Paradoxical intention   In Franklian terms, it "means that the patient is encouraged to do, or wish to happen, the very things he fears. … It lends itself to the short-term treatment of obsessive-compulsive and phobic patients."

Paranoia   Mental disorder characterized by unrealistic feelings of persecution, grandiosity, and suspicious attitude toward others.

Parataxic   Sullivan's terms for the mode of cognition characterized by attribution of cause and effect when none is present; private language not consensually validated (I.e., not able to be accurately communicated to others).

Parsimony   Criterion of a useful theory, which states that when two theories are equal on other criteria, the simpler one is preferred.

Peak experience A classic concept of Maslow used to refer to an intense, mystical experience often characteristic of self-actualizing people, but not limited to them.

Perceptual-conscious   In Freud's thought, the system that perceives external stimuli through sight, sound, taste, etc., and communicates them to the conscious system.

Person of tomorrow   Rogers used this phrase to refer to the psychologically healthy individual in the process of evolving into all that he or she can become.

Person-centered   The theory of personality founded by Carl Rogers as an outgrowth of his client-centered psychotherapy.

Persona   Jungian archetype that represents that side of personality one shows to the rest of the wold. Also, the mask worn by ancient Roman actors in the Greek theater, and thus the root of the word "personality."

Personal unconscious   Jung's term for those repressed experiences which pertain exclusively to one particular individual; opposed to the collective unconscious which pertains to unconscious experiences that originate with repeated experiences of our ancestors.

Personality A universal concept referring to all those relatively permanent traits, dispositions, or characteristics within the individual, which give some degree of consistency to that person's behavior. Traits may be unique, common to some groups or culture, or shared by the entire species. At present, no one definition of personality is accepted universally and every major school of psychotherapy has produced its own.

Personifications   Sullivan used this term to apply to images a person has of self or others, such as "good-mother," "Bad-mother," "good-me," and "bad-me."

Phallic phase   Freud's term for the third and latest stage of the infantile period, this period is characterized by the Oedipus complex. Though anatomical differences between the sexes are responsible for important differences in the male and female Oedipal periods, Freud used the term phallic phase to signify both the male and the female developmental stage. He has been roundly criticized by the feminist psychoanalists of the day.

Pleasure principle   Freud used this term to refer to the motivation of the id to seek immediate reduction of tension through the gratification of instinctual drives.

Positive regard Rogers used this term to refer to the need to be loved, liked, or accepted by another.

Positive reinforcer   Any stimulus which, when added to a situation, increases the probability that a given behavior will occur.

Preconscious   Freud meant by this term those mental elements which are currently not in awareness, but which can become conscious with varying degrees of difficulty.

Primary narcissism   Freud meant the infant's investment of libido upon its own ego; self-love or autoerotic behavior of the infant.

Primary process   Freud's term which refers to the id, which houses the primary motivators of behavior called instincts.

Progression   Jung's term for the forward flow of psychic energy. Involves the extraverted attitude and movement toward adaptation to the external world.

Projection   A defense mechanism whereby the ego reduces anxiety by attributing an unwanted impulse to another person or object.

Phototoxic   Primitive, presymbolic, undifferentiated mode of experience which cannot be communicated to others.

Psychoanalysis   Theory of personality, developed by Freud and the Freudian school called by this name, and a recognized mode of psychotherapy.

Psychodynamic   Loosely defined term usually referring to those psychological theories which heavily emphasize unconscious motivation. The theories of Freud, Adler, Jung, and Sullivan are usually considered to be psychodynamic.

Psychoid unconscious   Jung's term for those elements in the unconscious which are not capable of becoming conscious.

Psychopathology   General term referring to various levels and types of mental disturbances or beahvior disorders, including neuroses, psychoses, and psychosomatic ailments.

Psychosis   Severe personality disorders, as opposed to the more mild neurotic reactions. Psychoses interfere seriously with the usual functions of life and include both organic brain disfunctions and functional or learned condictions.

Quaternary   A Jungian term used to refer to an archetype symbolized by figures with four equal dies or four elements.

Rational functions   Jung's term for the methods of dealing with the world which involve thinking and feeling, i.e., valuing.

Reaction formation   A defense mechanism characterized by the repression of one impulse and the adoption of the exact opposite form of behavior. Reactive behavior is ordinarily exaggerated and ostentatious.

Reality principle   Freud's term used to refer to the go, which must realistically arbitrate the conflicting demands of the id, the superego, and the external world.

Regression   Freud's term for a defense mechanism whereby the person returns to a stage previously catheter by libido in order to protect the ego against anxiety; return to an earlier time in life, usually childhood.

Regression   Jung's term for the backward flow of psychic energy. Regression involves the introverted attitude and movement towards adaptation to the internal world.

Repetition compulsion   Freud used this concept to refer to the tendency of the instinct, especially the death instinct, to repeat or recreate an earlier condition, particularly one that was frightening or anxiety-arousing.

Repression   Freud's term for the forcing of unwanted, anxiety-laden experiences into the unconscious in order to defend the person against the pain of that anxiety.

Resacralization   Maslow developed this concept for the process of returning respect, joy, awe, rapture, etc., to an experience in order that the experience is more subjective and personal.

Sadistic-anal phase   Freud used this concept to refer to the anal phase, this is the second stage of the infantile period and is characterized by attempts to gain pleasure from the execretory function and such related behaviors as destroying or losing objects, stubbornness, neatness, and miserliness. Corresponds roughly to the second year of life.

Safeguarding tendencies   A dominant concept in Adlerian psychology, the term is used to refer to the protective mechanisms such as aggression, withdrawal, etc., which maintain exaggerated feelings of superiority.

Schizophrenia   Psychotic disorder characterized by fundamental disturbances in perception of reality, severe apathy, and loss of affect.

Secondary narcissism   Freudian concept referring to self-love or autoerotic behavior in an adolescent.

Secondary reinforcement   Learned reinforcement. If a previously ineffective event, for example money, increases the likelihood that learning will take place, then that event is a secondary reinforcer.

Selective inattention   A classic term developed by Sullivan to refer to the control of focal awareness, which involves a refusal to see those things one does not wish to see or a refusal to hear things one wishes not to hear.

Self   In Jungian psychology, the most comprehensive of all archetypes, including the whole of personality, though it is mostly unconscious. The self is often symbolized by the mandala motif.

Self-accusation   Adlerian safeguarding tendency whereby the person aggresses indirectly against others through self-torture and guilt.

Self-actualization   Maslow's classic concept referring to the highest level of human motivation characterized by full development of all one's capacities.

Self-regard   Roger developed this term to refer to the need to accept, like, or love oneself.

Self-system   Sullivan's term for the complex of dynamisms that protect the person from anxiety and maintain interpersonal security.

Self-transcendence In Franklian psychology, "self-transcendence is our ability to reach beyond ourselves to people we love or to causes that are important to us (Lukas)." "Self-transcendence is the essence of existence. Being human is being directed to something other than itself" according to Frankl.

Shadow   Jungian archetype representing the inferior or dark side of personality.

Social interest   An Adlerian term for the translation of the German, *Gemeinschaftsgefuhl,* meaning a community feeling or a sense of feeling at one with all human beings.

Solicitude   Adlerian safeguarding tendency whereby the

individual depreciates others and receives an inflated feeling of superiority by acting as if other people are incapable of caring from themselves.

Somnolent detachment Sullivan's term for the dynamism that protects the person from increasingly strong and painful effects of severe anxiety.

Standing still Adlerian term for the safeguarding tendency characterized by lack of action as a means of avoiding failure.

Stereotypes Sullivan used this term to refer to imaginary traits attributed to a group of people.

Style of life Adler's terms for a person's individuality expressing itself in any circumstance or environment; the "flavor" of a person's life.

Subception A term developed by Rogers to refer to the process of perceiving stimuli without an awareness of the perception.

Sublimation A defense mechanism that involves the repression of the genital aim of Eros and its substitution by a cultural or social aim.

Successive approximations Procedure used to shape an organism's behavior; entails the rewarding of behaviors as they become closer and closer to the target behavior.

Superego Freud's classic term for that province of the mind which refers to the moral or ethical processes of personality. The superego has two subsystems — the conscience, which tells us what is wrong, and the ego-ideal, which tells us what is right.

Superiority complex Adler's terms used to refer to the exaggerated and unrealistic feelings of personal superiority as an overcompensation for unusually strong feelings of inferiority.

Suppression the blocking or inhibiting of an activity by either a conscious act of the will or by an outside agent such as parents or other authority figures. Not to be confused with *repression*, which is the unconscious blocking of anxiety-producing experiences.

Syntaxic Sullivan's well-developed concept used to refer to the consensually validated experiences. As the highest level of cognition, syntaxic experiences can be accurately communicated to others, usually through language.

Taoist attitude An adapted term developed by Maslow to refer to the no interfering, passive, receptive attitude that includes awe and wonder toward that which is observed.

Tenderness Sullivan used this term to refer to the tension within the mothering one, which is aroused by the manifest needs of the infant. Within the child tenderness is felt as the need to receive care.

Terror Sullivan's term for the experience of absolute or complete tension.

Theory A scientific theory is a set of related assumptions from which, by logical deductive reasoning, testable hypotheses can be drawn.

Thinking By this term, Jung meant a rational function that tells us the meaning of a sensation that originates either from the external world (extraverted) or from the internal or subjective world (introverted).

Third Force Somewhat vague terms referring to those approaches to psychology which have reacted against the psychodynamic and behaviorist theories of Freud, Jung, Adler and Skinner and all those in between them. Rogers and Frankl belong to the Third Force but some would argue that Erikson and Maslow belong to the psychodynamic school. Since no one pays dues to belong to one or the other, the question is essentially irrelevant.

Threat Roger's term for the results from the perception of an experience that is inconsistent with one's organismic self.

Transference Freud developed the term but many schools now use it to refer to the strong, underserved feelings the patient develops towad the analyst during the course of treatment. This feeling may be either sexual or hostile and stems from the patient's earlier experiences with parents.

Transformation Psychotherapeutic approach used by Jung wherein the therapist is transformed into a healthy individual who can aid the patient in establishing a philosophy of life.

Types Jung's classification of people based on the two-dimensional scheme of attitudes and functions. The two attitudes of extraversion and introversion and the four functions of thinking, feeling, sensing, and intuiting combine to produce eight possible types.

Unconditional positive regard A Rogerian term for the need to be accepted and prized by another without any restrictions or qualifications. One of three "necessary and sufficient" therapeutic conditions.

Unconscious Freud meant all those mental elements of which a person is unaware. Two levels of the unconscious are the unconscious proper and the preconscious. Unconscious ideas can become conscious only through great resistance and difficulty.

Undoing A Freudian defense mechanism, closely related to repression, involving the ego's attempt to do away with unpleasant experiences and their consequences by an expenditure of energy on compulsive ceremonial activities.

Vulnerable A Rogerian term for a condition that exists when people are unaware of the discrepancy between their organism selves and their experiences. Vulnerable people often behave in ways incomprehensible to themselves and to others.

Will-to-meaning "According to logo therapy," says Frankl, "the striving to find a meaning in one's life is the primary motivational force in man." This is in opposition to the will-to-pleasure in Freudian psychology and the will-to-power in Adler's thought.

Withdrawal Adler's term for safeguarding one's exaggerated sense of superiority by establishing a distance between oneself and one's problems.

BIBLIOGRAPHY
(biographical/primary/secondary sources)

BIOGRAPHICAL SOURCES IN ORDER OF THEORIST

Sigmund Freud

Freud: A Life for Our Time by Peter Gay. NY: W. W. Norton & Company, 1988.

Alfred Adler
The Drive for Self: Alfred Adler and theFounding of Individual Psychology by Edward Hoffman. NY: Addison-Wesley Publishing, 1994.

Carl Gustav Jung
Carl Gustav Jung by Frank McLynn. NY: St. Martin's Griffin, 1996.

Viktor Frankl
When Life Calls Out to Us: The Love and Lifework Of Viktor and Elly Frankl by Haddon Klingberg, Jr.NY: Doubleday, 2001.

Abraham Maslow
The Right to be Human: A Biography of Abraham Maslow by Edward Hoffman. Los Angeles: JeremyP. Tarcher, Inc., 1988.

Erik Erikson
Identity's Architect: A Biography of Erik H. Erikson By Lawrence J. Friedman. Cambridge, MA: Harvard University Press, 1999.

Carl Rogers
On Becoming Carl Rogers by Howard Kirschenbaum. NY: Delacorte Press, 1979.

Harry Stack Sullivan
Psychiatrist of America: The Life of Harry Stack Sullivan BY
Helen Swick Perry. Cambridge, MA: The Belknap Press of
Harvard University Press, 1982.

PRIMARY SOURCES IN ORDER OF THEORISTS

SIGMUND FREUD
Studies on Hysteria (with Josef Breuer) (*Studien über Hysterie,*
1895)

With Robert Fliess: *The Complete Letters of Sigmund Freud to
Wilhelm Fliess, 1887-1904*, Publisher: Belknap Press, 1986, ISBN
0674154215

The Interpretation of Dreams (*Die Traumdeutung,* 1899 [1900])

The Psychopathology of Everyday Life (*Zur Psychopathologie des
Alltagslebens,* 1901)

Three Essays on the Theory of Sexuality (*Drei Abhandlungen zur
Sexualtheorie,* 1905)

Jokes and their Relation to the Unconscious (*Der Witz und seine
Beziehung zum Unbewußten,* 1905)

Totem and Taboo (*Totem und Tabu,* 1913)

On Narcissism (*Zur Einführung des Narzißmus,* 1914)

Beyond the Pleasure Principle (*Jenseits des Lustprinzips,* 1920)
The Ego and the Id (*Das Ich und das Es,* 1923)

The Future of an Illusion (*Die Zukunft einer Illusion,* 1927)

Civilization and Its Discontents (*DasUnbehagen in der Kultur,*1930)

Moses and Monotheism (*Der Mann Moses und die monotheistische Religion*, 1939)

An Outline of Psycho-Analysis (*Abriß der Psychoanalyse*, 1940)

A Phylogenetic Fantasy: Overview of the Transference Neuroses translated by Axel Hoffer by Peter Hoffer, Harvard University Press.

ALFRED ADLER

The Practice and Theory of Individual Psychology (1927)

Understanding Human Nature (1927)

What Life Could Mean to You (1931)

In his lifetime, Adler published more than 300 books and articles. The Alfred Adler Institute of Northwestern Washington has recently published the first ten of the twelve-volume set of *The Collected Clinical Works of Alfred Adler*, covering his writings from 1898-1937. An entirely new translation of Adler's magnum opus, *The Neurotic Character*, is featured in Volume 1.

Volume 1 : The Neurotic Character — 1907
Volume 2 : Journal Articles 1898-1909
Volume 3 : Journal Articles 1910-1913
Volume 4 : Journal Articles 1914-1920
Volume 5 : Journal Articles 1921-1926
Volume 6 : Journal Articles 1927-1931
Volume 7 : Journal Articles 1931-1937
Volume 8 : *Lectures to Physicians & Medical Students*
Volume 9 : *Case Histories*
Volume 10 : *Case Readings & Demonstrations*
Volume 11 : *Education for Prevention*
Volume 12 : *The General System of Individual Psychology*

The Individual Psychology of Alfred Adler. H. L. Ansbacher and R. R. Ansbacher (Eds.). New York: Harper Torch books (1956).

CARL GUSTAV JUNG

Works arranged by original publication date if known:

Psychiatric Studies. The Collected Works of C. G. Jung Vol. 1. 1953, ed. Michael Fordham, London: Routledge & Kegan Paul, and Princeton, N.J.: Bollingen. (This was the first of 18 volumes plus separate bibliography and index. Not including revisions the set was completed in 1967.)

Studies in Word Association. London: Routledge & K. Paul. (contained in *Experimental Researches*, Collected Works Vol. 2).

The Psychology of Dementia Praecox. (1907; 2nd ed. 1936) New York: Nervous and Mental Disease Publ. Co. (Contained in *The Psychogenesis of Mental Disease*, Collected Works Vol. 3. This is the disease now known as schizophrenia).

The Psychogenesis of Mental Disease. 1991 ed. London: Routledge. (Collected Works Vol. 3) (1907)

Psychology of the Unconscious : a study of the transformations and symbolisms of the libido, a contribution to the history of the evolution of thought. London: Kegan Paul Trench Trubner. (revised in 1952 as *Symbols of Transformation*, Collected Works Vol 15, (1912).

Collected Papers on Analytical Psychology (2nd ed.). London: Balliere Tindall & Cox. (contained in *Freud and Psychoanalysis*, Collected Works Vol. 4) (1917)

Two Essays on Analytical Psychology (1966 revised 2nd ed. Collected Works Vol. 7). London: Routledge, (1917, 1928).

Psychological Types, or, *The Psychology of Individuation.* London: Kegan Paul Trench Trubner. (Collected Works Vol.6, (1921).

Contributions to Analytical Psychology. London: Routledge & Kegan Paul, (1928).

The Psychology of Kundalini Yoga: notes of a seminar by C.G. Jung. 1996 ed. Princeton, N.J.: Princeton University Press, (1932).

Modern Man in Search of a Soul. London: Kegan Paul Trench Trubner, (1955 ed. Harvest Books, (1933).

The Archetypes and the Collective Unconscious. (1981 2nd ed. Collected Works Vol.9 Part 1), Princeton, N.J.: Bolingen, (1934–1954).

Psychology and Religion The Terry Lectures. New Haven: Yale University Press. (contained in *Psychology and Religion: West and East* Collected Works Vol. 11, (1938).

The Integration of the Personality. London: Routledge and Kegan Paul, (1940).

Psychology and Alchemy (2nd ed. 1968 Collected Works Vol. 12). London: Routledge, (1944).

Essays on Contemporary Events. London: Kegan Paul, (1947).
On the Nature of the Psyche. 1988 ed. London: Ark Paperbacks. (contained in Collected Works Vol. 8), (1947, revised 1954).

Foreword, pp. xxi-xxxix (19 pages), to Wilhelm/Baynes translation of *The I Ching or Book of Changes*. Bollingen Edition XIX, Princeton University Press.(contained in Collected Works Vol. 11), (1949).

Aion: Researches into the Phenomenology of the Self (Collected Works Vol. 9 Part 2). Princeton, N.J.: Bollingen, (1951).

Synchronicity: An Acausal Connecting Principle. 1973 2nd ed. Princeton, N.J.: Princeton University Press, (contained in Collected Works Vol. 8), (1952).

Mysterium Coniunctionis: An Inquiry into the Separation and Synthesis of Psychic Opposites in Alchemy. London: Routledge. (2nd ed. 1970 Collected Works Vol. 14), (1965). This was Jung's last book length work, completed when he was eighty.

The Undiscovered Self (Present and Future). 1959 ed. New York:
American Library. 1990 ed. Bollingen, (50 p. essay, also contained in
collected Works Vol. 10), (1957).

Psyche and Symbol: A Selection from the Writings of C.G. Jung.
Garden City, N.Y.: Doubleday, (1958).

Basic Writings. New York: Modern Library, (1959).

Memories, Dreams, Reflections. London: Collins. This is Jung's
autobiography, recorded and edited by Aniela Jaffe, (1962).

Conversations with Carl Jung and Reactions from Ernest Jones.
New York: Van Nostrand, (1964).

Man and His Symbols. Garden City, N.Y.: Doubleday, (1964).

*The Practice of Psychotherapy: Essays on the Psychology of the
Transference and other Subjects* (Collected Works Vol. 16).
Princeton, N.J.: Princeton University Press, (1966).

The Development of Personality. 1991 ed. London: Routledge.
Collected Works Vol. 17, (1967).

Four Archetypes; Mother, Rebirth, Spirit, Trickster. Princeton, N.J.:
Princeton University Press. (contained in Collected Works Vol. 9 part
1), (1970).

Dreams. Princeton, N.J.: Princeton University Press (compilation
from Collected Works Vols. 4, 8, 12, 16), (1974).

The Portable Jung. a compilation, New York: Penguin Books,
(1976).

(1978). *Abstracts of the Collected Works of C.G. Jung.* Washington,
D.C.: U.S. Govt. Printing Office, (1978).

The Essential Jung. a compilation, Princeton, N.J.: Princeton
University Press, Jung, (1983).

Psychology and the East. London: Ark. (contained in Collected Works Vol. 11), (1986).

Dictionary of Analytical Psychology. London: Ark Paperbacks, (1987).

Psychology and Western Religion. London: Ark Paperbacks. (contained in Collected Works Vol. 11), (1988).

The World Within C.G. Jung in his own words [videorecording]. New York, NY: Kino International : Dist. by Insight Media, (1990).

Psychological Types (a revised ed.). London: Routlege, (1991).

Jung on Active Imagination. Princeton, N.J.: Princeton University Press, (1997).

Jung's *Seminar on Nietzsche's Zarathustra* (Abridged ed.). Princeton, N.J.: Princeton University Press, (1998).

Atom and Archetype : The Pauli/Jung Letters, 1932-1958, Princeton, N.J.: Princeton University Press, (2001).

The Earth Has a Soul: the nature writings of C.G. Jung. Berkeley, Calif.: North Atlantic Books. Anthony Stevens. "Jung, A Very Short Introduction" (1994) An early writing by Jung, dating from around 1917, was his poetic work, *The Seven Sermons To The Dead* (Full Text). Written in the persona of the 2nd century religious teacher Basilides of Alexandria, it explores ancient religious and spiritual themes, including those of gnosticism. This work is included in some editions of *Memories, Dreams, Reflections, (*2002).

VIKTOR FRANKL

Man's Search for Meaning. An Introduction to Logotherapy, Boston: Beacon and Random House / Rider, London 2004, also Washington Square Press; (Softcover, December 1997)

On the Theory and Therapy of Mental Disorders. An Introduction to Logotherapy and Existential Analysis, Translated by James M. DuBois. Brunner-Routledge, London-New York, 2004.

Psychotherapy and Existentialism. Selected Papers on Logotherapy, New York: Simon & Schuster.

The Will to Meaning. Foundations and Applications of Logotherapy, New York: New American Library.

Man's Search for Ultimate Meaning. (A revised and extended edition of The Unconscious God; with a Foreword by Swanee Hunt). Perseus Book Publishing, New York, 1997; Paperback edition: Perseus Book Group; New York, July 2000.

ABRAHAM MASLOW

A Theory of Human Motivation (originally published in *Psychological Review*, 1943, Vol. 50 #4, pp. 370-396).

Motivation and Personality (1st edition: 1954).

Religions, Values and Peak-experiences, Columbus, Ohio: Ohio State University Press, 1964.

Eupsychian Management, 1965; republished as *Maslow on Management*, 1998.

The Psychology of Science: A Reconnaissance, New York: Harper & Row, 1966; Chapel Hill: Maurice Bassett, 2002.

Toward a Psychology of Being, (2nd edition, 1968).

The Farther Reaches of Human Nature, 1971.

ERIK ERIKSON

Childhood and Society (1950)

Young Man Luther. A Study in Psychoanalysis and History (1958)

Identity: Youth and Crisis (1968)

Gandhi's Truth: On the Origin of Militant Nonviolence (1969)

Adulthood (edited book, 1978)

Vital Involvement in Old Age (with J.M. Erikson and H. Kivnick, 1986)

The Life Cycle Completed (with J.M. Erikson, 1987)

Identity and the Life Cycle. Selected Papers (1959)

A Way of Looking at Things: Selected Papers 1930-1980 (Editor: S.P. Schlien, 1915)

The Erik Erikson Reader (Editor: Robert Coles, 2001)

Erikson on Development in Adulthood: New Insights from the Unpublished Papers (Carol Hren Hoare, 2002)

Erik Erikson Worked For His Life, Work, and Significance (Kit Welchman, 2000)

Identity's Architect: A Biography of Erik H. Erikson (Lawrence J. Friedman, 1999)

Erik H. Erikson: The Power and Limits of a Vision, N.Y., The Free Press (Paul Roazen, 1976)

"Everybody Rides the Carousel" (documentary film) (Hubley, 1976)

Erik H. Erikson: the Growth of His Work (Robert Coles, 1970)

Ideas and Identities: The Life and Work of Erik Erikson (Robert S. Wallerstein & Leo Goldberger, eds., [IUP, 1998])

CARL ROGERS

Clinical Treatment of the Problem Child, (1939).

Counseling and Psychotherapy: Newer Concepts in Practice, (1942).

Client-centered Therapy: Its Current Practice, Implications and Theory. London: Constable, (1951).

"A Theory of Therapy, Personality and Interpersonal Relationships as Developed in the Client-centered Framework." In (ed.) S. Koch, *Psychology: A Study of a Science. Vol. 3: Formulations of the Person and the Social Context*. New York: McGraw Hill, (1959).

On Becoming a Person: A Therapist's View of Psychotherapy. London: Constable, (1961).

Freedom to Learn: A View of What Education Might Become. (1st ed.) Columbus, Ohio: Charles Merrill, (1969).

On Encounter Groups. New York: Harper and Row, (1970).

On Personal Power: Inner Strength and Its Revolutionary Impact, (1977).

A Way of Being. Boston: Houghton Mifflin, (1980).

HARRY STACK SULLIVAN

Conceptions of Modern Psychiatry: The First William Alanson

White Memorial Lectures, NY: W. W. Norton & co., 1953.

Personal Psychopathology, NY: W. W. Norton & co., 1972.

The Interpersonal Theory of Psychiatry, NY: W. W. Norton & Co., 1953.

The Psychiatric Interview, NY: W. W. Norton & Co., 1954.

Clinical Studies in Psychiatry, NY: W. W. Norton & Co., 1956.

Schizophrenia as a Human Process, NY: W. W. Norton & Co., 1962.

The Fusion of Psychiatry and Social Science, NY: W. W. Norton & Co., 1964.

SECONDARY SOURCES

Note: Because of the massive amount of scholarship related to each of these theorists in terms of published works, I have chosen here simply to mention those that have been of particular relevance to me in the development of this book and my life's work in this field. There is no claim either to thoroughness or completeness but merely to personal representational preferences.

Amada, Gerald. *A Guide to Psychotherapy* (NY: Madison Books, 1985).

Chan, Henry A. *the Mediator as Human Being: From a Study of Major Concepts of Sigmund Freud, Carl Jung, Erik Erikson, and Abraham Maslow* (Lima, OH: Wyndham Hall Press, 2005).

Feist, Jess. *Theories of Personality* (NY: Holt, Rinehart and Winston, 1985.

Graber, Ann V. *Viktor Frankl's Logotherapy: Method of Choice in Ecumenical Pastoral Psychology, 2ⁿᵈ edition* (Lima, OH: Wyndham Hall Press, 2004).

Hall, Calvin S. and Gardner Lindzey. *Theories of Personality* (NY: John Wiley & Sons, 1957).

Hjelle, Larry A. and Daniel J. Ziegler, *Personality Theories: Basic Assumptions, Research, and Applications* (NY: McGraw-Hill Book Company, 1976).

Jones, Ernst. *The Life and Work of Sigmund Feud* (3 volumes) (NY: Basic Books, 1957).

Kendler, Howard H. *Historical Foundations of Modern Psychology* (Chicago, IL: The Dorsey Press, 1987.

Lundin, Robert W. *Theories and Systems of Psychology*, Third Edition (Lexington, MA: D. C. Heath and Co., 1985).

Millon, Theodore. *Theories of Personality and Psychopathology*, Third Edition (NY: Holt, Rinehart and Winston, 1983).

Monte, Christopher F. *Beneath the Mask: An Introduction to Theories of Personality* (NY: Holt, Rinehart and Winton, 1987).

Reber, Arthur S. *The Penguin Dictionary of Psychology* (NY: Penguin Books, 1985).

Zeig, Jeffrey K., Edtior. *The Evolution of Psychotherapy* (NY: Brunner/Mazel, Publishers, 1987).

About The Author

John Henry Morgan, Ph.D.(Hartford), D.Sc.(/CASLondon), Psy.D.(FH/Oxford) is the Karl Mannheim Professor of the History and Philosophy of the Social Sciences at the Graduate Theological Foundation where he has been president since 1982. He is also the Sir Julia Huxley Research Professor at Cloverdale College as well as being a Senior Fellow of Foundation House/Oxford. In 1972, he was elected the first president of the Connecticut Society for Religion and Health, a professional body of psychiatrists and pastors working together on mental health issues relevant to the general public. He has held postdoctoral appointments to Harvard, Yale, and Princeton and was a National Science Foundation Science Faculty Fellow at the University of Notre Dame. Following a postdoctoral appointment at the Hebrew Union College/Jewish Institute of Religion where he worked with the late Rabbi Samuel Sandmel, Dr. Morgan was sub-sequently appointed three times a postdoctoral Research Fellow at the University of Chicago. Recently, he was appointed Postdoctoral Visiting Scholar at New York University. In 1986, he established and was Director of the Harry Stack Sullivan Research Institute of Social Psychiatry at Bethel College in Indiana where he was also Professor of Psychology and Department chair. He teaches a doctoral seminar at Oxford University where he has been a member of the Board of Studies of the summer theology program since 1995. Dr. Morgan is the author/editor of over thirty books in the history and philosophy of the social sciences and has been elected to membership in the American Psychological Association, the American Philosophical Association, the American Sociological Association, the American Anthropological Association, and to the Advisory Board of the Centre for the Study of Religion and Public Life at the University of Oxford. Recently, he has been invited to teach a course at Madingley Hall, Cambridge University (UK).

Index

A

activity 55, 63, 88, 150, 186
actualizing 104, 123, 160, 166, 167
aesthetic Needs 124
aesthetic needs 127
aggression 39-41, 45, 71, 72
analytical Psychology 75, 78, 80, 84, 90
analytical psychology 19, 28, 54, 69, 82
anima 89, 92
anxiety 30, 40, 46, 64, 103, 110, 125, 177, 181, 187, 192, 194
archetypes 69, 81, 82, 84, 89, 91, 92, 93, 141, 144
attitude 30, 41, 46, 55-59, 63, 73, 85, 87, 103,
111, 145, 156, 168, 185, 187

B

B-Values 127
basic anxiety 125
behaviorism 12-15, 18, 114-117, 119, 122, 165, 168, 175, 195

C

client-centered therapy 159, 162, 195
cognitive needs 124, 127
collective unconscious 209
complex 15, 40, 48, 90, 92
condition of worth 171, 172
conscience 39, 40, 41, 46, 103, 105, 108
conscious 18, 42, 43, 44, 70, 81, 89, 91, 104, 169, 170, 172

D

death instinct 39
defense mechanisms 173
defensiveness 166
dynamism 186, 187

E

ego 18, 32, 34, 38-41, 45, 46, 47, 81, 89-93, 139-149,152
ego-ideal 46
empathy 165
empirical 44, 91
erogenous zones 48
excuses 64
existential 18, 46, 101, 130, 164, 174, 196
existential analysis 98
existential frustration 101
existential vacuum 108-110
extraversion 85, 89

F

feeling 13, 69, 73, 87
fiction 65
fixation 48

H

hierarchy of needs 115, 122, 124, 126
humanistic psychology 113, 115, 118, 121, 122, 123, 168, 175
hysteria 23, 25, 79

I

id 18, 33, 34, 45, 46, 90, 143
ideal self 169
incongruence 164, 170, 177
individual psychology 51, 55, 57, 61, 68, 70, 119
individuation 93
inferiority complex 57, 58, 60, 61, 65
instinct 38, 45, 70, 108, 110
intimacy 150, 186, 187, 192
intuition 85, 87
isolation 81, 150

L

libido 33, 36, 80
life instinct 39
logotherapy 18, 95, 100, 102, 107, 196
lust 186, 187, 192

M

malevolence 186
masculine protest 71
maturity 22, 33, 34, 107, 168

N

neurasthenia 79
neurosis 30, 36, 41, 55, 78, 101, 102, 104, 110

O

oedipus complex 40, 48

P

paradoxical intention 108, 110, 111
parataxic 187
peak experience 121, 130
person-centered 18
persona 89, 92
personal unconscious 81, 82, 84, 89, 90
personality 12, 13, 45, 60, 65, 70, 77, 85
personifications 186-187
pleasure principle 30, 35, 39
positive regard 164, 165, 169, 170, 177
preconscious 43
projection 39
psychoanalysis 18, 20, 21, 42, 48, 69, 79, 115, 158, 181
psychodynamic 12, 49, 115
Psychopathology 28
psychosis 36

R

reality principle 33, 35, 39, 46, 47

S

schizophrenia 184
self-actualization 89, 93, 116, 118, 126, 167
self-system 186, 187
shadow 89, 92, 93
social interest 69, 72
solicitude 65
stereotypes 187
style of life 59, 68, 69, 70, 73
sublimation 38
superego 18, 41, 166
suppression 184
syntaxic 187, 188, 192, 194

T

third force 116, 118, 122, 139, 176, 195
threat 172, 173
transference 18, 50, 186
transformation 200

U

unconditional positive regard 164, 171, 177
undoing 170

V

vulnerable 177

W

will-to-meaning 101, 102

www.ingramcontent.com/pod-product-compliance
Lightning Source LLC
Chambersburg PA
CBHW021617270326
41931CB00008B/737